FUNDAMENTALS OF
RISK MANAGEMENT

FOR

PROJECT MANAGERS

AND

BUSINESS OWNERS

MARION PARKER

Copyright © 2024 by Marion Parker

All Rights Reserved.

Executive Editor: Rachel Zhang

First Edition: July 2024.

No parts of this publication may be reproduced, distributed, or transmitted in any form or by any means, including photocopying, recording, or other electronic or mechanical methods, or by any information storage and retrieval system without the prior written permission of the author.

The information contained within this book is strictly for educational purposes. If you wish to apply ideas contained in this book, you are taking full responsibility for your actions.

PMBOK and PMP are registered marks of the Project Management Institute, Inc.

"Risk comes from not knowing what you're doing."
— Warren Buffet

TABLE OF CONTENTS

0 Preface 7
1 Introduction to Risk Management 9
    1.1 Understanding Risk 9
    1.2 Importance of Risk Management in Business 16
    1.3 Risk Management vs. Crisis Management 19
    1.4 Key Terms and Definitions 24
2 Frameworks and Standards in Risk Management 39
    2.1 ISO 31000 39
    2.2 COSO Framework 43
    2.3 PMBOK Guide on Risk Management 48
    2.4 Industry-Specific Standards 55
3 Risk Identification 60
    3.1 Techniques for Identifying Risks 60
        3.1.1 Brainstorming 60
        3.1.2 Delphi Technique 61
        3.1.3 SWOT Analysis 63
        3.1.4 Expert Interviews 64
    3.2 Common Sources of Risk 65
    3.3 Risk Register Development 68
4 Risk Assessment 71
    4.1 Qualitative Risk Assessment 71
    4.2 Quantitative Risk Assessment 74
        4.2.1 Monte Carlo Simulation 76
        4.2.2 Decision Tree Analysis 77
        4.2.3 Sensitivity Analysis 80
5 Risk Prioritization 84
    5.1 Risk Ranking Methods 84
    5.2 Risk Appetite and Tolerance 95
    5.3 Prioritizing Risks in the Context of Business Objectives 102
6 Risk Response Planning 104
    6.1 Negative Risks Responses 104

      6.1.1 Risk Avoidance 104

      6.1.2 Risk Mitigation 105

      6.1.3 Risk Transfer 106

      6.1.4 Risk Acceptance 107

  6.2 Positive Risks Responses 108

      6.2.1 Risk Exploitation 108

      6.2.2 Risk Enhancement 108

      6.2.3 Risk Sharing 109

      6.2.4 Risk Acceptance 110

  6.3 Contingency Planning 111

7 Implementing Risk Management Strategies 112

  7.1 Assigning Risk Owners 112

  7.2 Developing Risk Action Plans 113

  7.3 Integrating Risk Management into Business Processes 114

8 Monitoring and Reviewing Risks 116

  8.1 Continuous Risk Monitoring 116

  8.2 Key Risk Indicators (KRIs) 117

  8.3 Periodic Risk Reviews 118

  8.4 Adjusting Risk Responses 119

9 Communication and Reporting 120

  9.1 Communicating Risk to Stakeholders 121

  9.2 Risk Reporting Tools and Techniques 122

  9.3 Building a Risk-Aware Culture 125

10 Advanced Topics in Risk Management 127

  10.1 Enterprise Risk Management (ERM) 127

  10.2 Cybersecurity Risk Management 131

  10.3 Risk Management in Agile Projects 133

  10.4 Risk Management and Regulatory Compliance 134

11 Tools and Technologies for Risk Management 137

  11.1 Risk Management Software 137

  11.2 Data Analytics in Risk Management 138

  11.3 Artificial Intelligence & Machine Learning in Risk Management ... 139

12 Final Thoughts 142

13 One Last Thing.. 144

0   Preface

Thank you for choosing this book. It is my sincere hope that it will enhance your skills in Risk Management and empower you to navigate uncertainties with confidence.

The overwhelming response to my first book on Contracts Management prompted me to consider your feedback for a follow-up focusing on Risk Management — another critical pillar for successfully steering any business venture.

This book has been crafted with dedication and a heartfelt desire to assist you in navigating the complexities of risk within your day-to-day operations. While our goal is to familiarize you with fundamental concepts, it's important to note that Risk Management is a nuanced discipline that demands continuous learning.

In today's fast-paced and ever-changing business environment, the ability to effectively manage risks can make the difference between success and failure. Whether you are a seasoned professional or new to the field, this book aims to provide you with practical insights and tools to identify, assess, and mitigate risks in your organization.

The structure of this book is designed to guide you step-by-step through the various aspects of risk management. Starting with an introduction to the basic principles and moving through to advanced topics, each chapter builds upon the previous one, offering a comprehensive understanding of the subject.

We begin with an overview of what risk management entails and its significance in the business context. From there, we explore established frameworks and standards that provide a foundation for effective risk management practices. You will learn various techniques for identifying risks, followed by methods for assessing and prioritizing them.

One of the key elements of this book is the practical application of risk response strategies. We cover both negative and positive risk responses, providing real-world examples to illustrate each approach. Additionally, we delve into the implementation of these strategies, emphasizing the importance of assigning risk owners and integrating risk management into your business processes.

Monitoring and reviewing risks is an ongoing process, and this book offers guidance on how to continuously track and adjust your risk responses. Effective communication and reporting are also crucial, and we discuss ways to build a risk-aware culture within your organization.

In the final sections, we explore advanced topics such as Enterprise Risk Management (ERM), cybersecurity risk management, and the application of risk management in agile projects. We also highlight the latest tools and technologies that can enhance your risk management capabilities.

As you embark on this journey, remember that risk management is not a one-time task but a continuous process that evolves with your business. Stay curious, stay informed, and always be prepared to adapt to new challenges.

Writing this book has been a personal journey for me, one that has deepened my appreciation for the intricate balance between risk and opportunity. I've poured my experiences, lessons learned, and insights into these pages, hoping to provide you with a resource that is both informative and inspiring.

Thank you for allowing me to be a part of your learning journey. I hope this book provides you with valuable insights and practical knowledge that you can apply in your professional life.

Happy risk management!

Warm regards,

Marion Parker

1 Introduction to Risk Management

1.1 Understanding Risk

Risk is an inherent aspect of any business endeavor or project. It represents the possibility that events or conditions may occur, impacting the objectives of the organization or project, either positively or negatively. Thus, understanding risk is the first step toward effective risk management.

Definition of Risk

Risk can be defined as the effect of uncertainty on objectives. It is often measured in terms of the <u>likelihood</u> of an event and the <u>consequences</u> of that event. In business and project management contexts, risks can come from various sources such as financial uncertainties, legal liabilities, strategic management errors, accidents, and natural disasters.

Key Characteristics of Risk

1. **Uncertainty**: At the core of risk is uncertainty. Uncertainty arises due to the <u>lack of complete information</u> about future events. This uncertainty can pertain to the likelihood of occurrence, timing, and impact of potential events.
2. **Potential for Both Negative and Positive Outcomes**: Traditionally, risk has been viewed in a negative light, often equated with potential loss or damage. However, in risk management, it's important to recognize that <u>risks can also present opportunities</u>. These opportunities can lead to positive outcomes, such as higher returns on investment, gaining competitive advantages, or achieving strategic goals faster.

OK so.. you are saying that not all risks are bad for the business?

Correct! Keep in mind that some risks can be positive and produce positive outcomes as can be linked to opportunities. In this case the strategies will try to get the most out of them.

3. **Relative Nature**: <u>The perception and impact of risk vary depending on the context</u>. What may be considered a high risk for one project or organization might be seen as a low risk for another. This relativity is influenced by factors such as the organization's risk appetite, the project's nature, and the environment in which they operate.

Types of Risks

There are 5 types of risks you should keep in mind:

1. **Strategic Risks**: These are risks that affect the long-term goals and strategies of an organization. Examples include changes in market conditions, competition, and regulatory changes.

   Example

   > *A company specializing in renewable energy solutions is heavily investing in solar panel technology. However, a major breakthrough in nuclear fusion technology makes it a more viable and*

> *cost-effective energy source, drastically changing market conditions and rendering the company's solar panel strategy less competitive.*

2. **Operational Risks**: These risks arise from the internal processes, systems, and people within an organization. Examples include equipment failure, supply chain disruptions, and human error.

    Example

    > *A manufacturing plant relies on a specific machine for its production line. One day, this critical piece of equipment fails unexpectedly, causing a halt in production. This disruption leads to delays in fulfilling customer orders, increasing operational costs due to the urgent need for repairs or replacements, and potentially losing customer trust due to delayed deliveries.*

3. **Financial Risks**: These involve risks related to the financial health of the organization, such as market risk, credit risk, liquidity risk, and currency risk.

    Example

    > *A multinational corporation has significant investments in various international markets. Sudden fluctuations in exchange rates due to political instability in one of the countries lead to substantial financial losses. Additionally, a major customer defaults on a large payment, impacting the company's cash flow and liquidity, and causing difficulties in meeting short-term financial obligations.*

4. **Compliance Risks**: These are risks associated with failing to comply with laws, regulations, and standards. They can result in legal penalties, financial forfeiture, and reputational damage.

   Example

   > A pharmaceutical company launches a new drug without fully adhering to the updated regulations set by the Food and Drug Administration (FDA). After an audit, the company is found non-compliant, resulting in legal penalties, a mandatory recall of the drug, significant financial losses, and a damaged reputation.

5. **Reputational Risks**: These risks pertain to the potential loss of reputation or standing within the industry or community. Reputational risks can arise from various sources, including poor customer service, product failures, and negative publicity.

   Example

   > A food company experiences a widespread contamination issue with one of its popular products, leading to numerous cases of food poisoning. The incident gains widespread media attention, causing public outrage and a significant loss of consumer trust. Even after resolving the issue, the company struggles to rebuild its reputation and regain market share.

The Risk Management Process

To effectively manage risk, a structured process is employed, typically involving the following steps:

1. **Risk Identification**: The process of finding, recognizing, and describing risks.
2. **Risk Assessment**: Evaluating the identified risks to understand their potential impact and likelihood.
3. **Risk Prioritization**: Ranking risks based on their assessed impact and likelihood to determine which risks need immediate attention.
4. **Risk Response Planning**: Developing strategies and actions to address the prioritized risks.
5. **Risk Monitoring and Review**: Continuously tracking the identified risks, reassessing them, and identifying new risks as the project or business evolves.

While we will explore the details later in the book, we find it helpful to introduce an example of the Risk Management Process now to provide you with a clear overview.

Example

---

1. Risk Identification

Risk Identified: The development team identifies a risk that a key third-party software component, which the new software product relies on, might become unavailable or unsupported during the project lifecycle.

2. Risk Assessment

Impact: If the third-party component becomes unavailable, it could significantly delay the project timeline as the team would need to find an alternative solution and integrate it into the existing codebase. This could also lead to increased costs and reduced product functionality.

Likelihood: After some research, the team discovers that the third-party vendor has a history of discontinuing products without much notice. The likelihood is therefore assessed as moderate.

3. Risk Prioritization

Priority: Based on the high impact and moderate likelihood, this risk is prioritized as high. It is deemed necessary to address this risk immediately to avoid major disruptions to the project.

4. Risk Response Planning

Response Strategy: The team develops the following strategies to address the risk:

Mitigation: Start identifying and evaluating alternative third-party components early in the project. This includes ensuring that these alternatives can meet the project's technical requirements and are from vendors with a stable track record.

Contingency Plan: Prepare for the potential transition by creating a flexible architecture that allows for easier integration of a new component. Allocate extra budget and time in the project plan for this potential change.

Monitoring: Establish regular communication with the third-party vendor to get early warnings about any potential discontinuation. Keep an eye on industry news and forums for any signs of changes regarding the third-party component.

5. Risk Monitoring and Review

Monitoring: The project manager sets up monthly reviews to monitor the status of the third-party component and the vendor's stability. The team stays updated with the latest news and changes from the vendor and is prepared to act on their contingency plan if any signals of discontinuation arise.

Review: During these reviews, the risk is reassessed based on any new information. If the vendor shows signs of instability or if the software

> *component is flagged for potential discontinuation, the team is ready to swiftly move to an alternative solution as outlined in the contingency plan.*

The Importance of Understanding Risk

Understanding risk is critical for several reasons:

- **Informed Decision-Making**: With a clear understanding of the risks involved, managers and stakeholders can make informed decisions, balancing potential rewards against potential losses.
- **Proactive Management**: Identifying and assessing risks early allows organizations to take proactive measures to mitigate or capitalize on these risks, rather than reacting to events as they occur.
- **Resource Allocation**: Knowing which risks pose the greatest threat or opportunity enables better allocation of resources to address these risks effectively.
- **Improved Performance**: By managing risks effectively, organizations can improve project outcomes, enhance operational efficiency, and achieve strategic objectives.

All in all…

Understanding risk involves recognizing its uncertain nature, potential impacts, and the context-specific factors that influence its perception and management. By comprehensively understanding risk, project managers and business owners can implement effective risk management practices to safeguard and enhance their organizational objectives.

1.2 Importance of Risk Management in Business

In the dynamic landscape of modern business, risk management plays a crucial role in ensuring the longevity, stability, and success of an organization. For business owners and project managers, understanding and implementing effective risk management practices is essential to safeguard their enterprises and projects. Risk management involves the identification, assessment, and prioritization of risks, followed by coordinated efforts to minimize, monitor, and control the probability or impact of unfortunate events. Here are several reasons why risk management is vital for business owners and project managers.

1. Protecting Business Assets

For business owners, <u>protecting the company's physical and intangible assets is paramount</u>. These assets include physical properties, intellectual property, human resources, and financial resources. By identifying potential threats to these assets and developing strategies to protect them, business owners can prevent significant losses and disruptions. Project managers also benefit from risk management by safeguarding project resources, ensuring that timelines and budgets are adhered to.

2. Enhancing Decision-Making

Business owners and project managers often face complex decisions. With a robust risk management framework, they have a clearer understanding of the potential risks and rewards associated with various business activities or project phases. This insight allows them to <u>make more informed decisions</u>, balancing opportunities against potential downsides. It leads to better strategic planning and resource allocation.

3. Ensuring Regulatory Compliance

Businesses must comply with numerous laws, regulations, and standards. <u>Failure to comply can result in legal penalties, financial losses, and reputational damage</u>. For business owners, risk management ensures that their company remains compliant with all relevant regulatory requirements, minimizing the risk of legal issues and fines. Project managers also need to consider regulatory compliance to avoid project delays and additional costs.

4. Building Resilience and Agility

In a rapidly changing business environment, <u>resilience and agility are critical</u> for both business owners and project managers. Risk management enables them to anticipate potential disruptions and develop contingency plans. This preparedness allows them to respond swiftly and effectively to unexpected events, maintaining operations and reducing downtime.

5. Protecting Reputation

A company's reputation is one of its <u>most valuable assets</u>. Negative events, such as data breaches, product recalls, or environmental accidents, can severely damage a company's reputation. Effective risk management helps business owners and project managers identify and mitigate risks that could harm the business's public image, ensuring sustained customer trust and loyalty.

6. Financial Stability

Financial risks, such as market fluctuations, credit risks, and liquidity risks, can significantly impact a business's financial stability. Risk management helps business owners identify and assess these financial risks, allowing them to implement measures to mitigate them. This can include diversifying investments, securing insurance, and maintaining adequate cash reserves. Project managers also need to manage financial risks to <u>keep projects within budget and avoid cost overruns.</u>

7. Supporting Growth and Innovation

Risk management is not just about avoiding or mitigating risks; it also involves identifying opportunities. For business owners, understanding and managing risks enables them to <u>pursue growth and innovation with greater confidence</u>. This proactive approach allows them to explore new markets, develop new products, and implement new technologies while managing potential downsides. Project managers can similarly use risk management to support innovative project approaches and methodologies.

8. Enhancing Operational Efficiency

Operational risks, such as equipment failure, supply chain disruptions, and human error, can lead to inefficiencies and increased costs. Risk management helps business owners and project managers identify and address these operational risks, improving efficiency and reducing costs. It also fosters a <u>culture of continuous improvement and vigilance</u> within the organization or project team.

9. Improving Stakeholder Confidence

Investors, customers, employees, and other stakeholders are more likely to have confidence in a business that <u>demonstrates effective risk management practices.</u> For business owners, this confidence can lead to increased investment, stronger customer relationships, and higher employee morale. Project managers can also benefit from improved stakeholder confidence, leading to better support, collaboration, and project success.

10. Long-Term Sustainability

Ultimately, the goal of risk management is to ensure the long-term sustainability of the business. For business owners, proactively managing risks can avoid or minimize the impact of adverse events, <u>ensuring continued operations and growth</u>. Project managers, on the other hand, can ensure that their projects contribute positively to the organization's long-term goals and sustainability.

All in all…

The importance of risk management in business cannot be overstated. For business owners and project managers, it is a fundamental aspect of responsible management and strategic planning. By identifying, assessing, and mitigating risks, they can protect assets, enhance decision-making, ensure regulatory compliance, build resilience, protect their reputation, maintain financial stability, support growth, improve operational efficiency, bolster stakeholder confidence, and ensure long-term sustainability. As such, risk management should be an integral part of every business strategy and project management plan.

1.3   RISK MANAGEMENT VS. CRISIS MANAGEMENT

For business owners and project managers, understanding the distinction between risk management and crisis management is crucial for maintaining stability and achieving long-term success. While both disciplines deal with uncertainty and adverse events, they differ significantly in their approaches, objectives, and timelines.

Understanding Risk Management

Risk Management is a <u>proactive process</u> aimed at identifying, assessing, and mitigating potential risks before they materialize. It focuses on reducing the likelihood and impact of negative events while also recognizing opportunities that can lead to positive outcomes. For business owners and project managers, effective risk management is integral to strategic planning and day-to-day operations.

As presented earlier in the book the key aspects of risk management include:

1. **Identification**: Recognizing potential risks that could affect business objectives or project outcomes. Business owners might identify risks related to market fluctuations, regulatory changes, or supply chain disruptions. Project managers might focus on risks related to project scope, budget, and timelines.
2. **Assessment**: Evaluating the likelihood and impact of identified risks. This involves both qualitative and quantitative analysis to prioritize risks based on their potential effect on the business or project.

3. **Mitigation**: Developing strategies to minimize the likelihood and impact of risks. Business owners might implement diversification strategies, secure insurance, or establish contingency plans. Project managers might allocate additional resources, adjust schedules, or incorporate risk mitigation measures into the project plan.
4. **Monitoring and Review**: Continuously tracking identified risks and reassessing them as new information becomes available. This allows business owners and project managers to adjust their risk management strategies in response to changing circumstances.

Understanding Crisis Management

Crisis Management, on the other hand, is a reactive process that deals with managing and resolving events that have already occurred and are causing significant disruption. It focuses on immediate response, damage control, and recovery to restore normal operations. For business owners and project managers, effective crisis management is essential for minimizing the impact of unforeseen events and ensuring rapid recovery.

Key aspects of crisis management include:

1. **Preparation**: Developing a crisis management plan that outlines roles, responsibilities, and procedures for handling various types of crises. Business owners might prepare for financial crises, data breaches, or natural disasters. Project managers might prepare for critical project failures or stakeholder conflicts.
2. **Response**: Implementing the crisis management plan when a crisis occurs. This involves mobilizing the crisis management team, communicating with stakeholders, and taking immediate action to contain the situation. Business owners and project managers must act quickly to mitigate damage and protect their organization or project.
3. **Recovery**: Restoring normal operations as quickly as possible. This includes assessing the damage, implementing recovery strategies, and providing support to affected employees or stakeholders. Business owners might focus on rebuilding customer trust and

financial stability. Project managers might focus on getting the project back on track and meeting revised objectives.
4. **Learning and Improvement**: Analyzing the crisis and the effectiveness of the response to identify lessons learned and improve future crisis management plans. Business owners and project managers should use this experience to strengthen their risk management and crisis management capabilities.

Comparing Risk Management and Crisis Management

For business owners and project managers, understanding the interplay between risk management and crisis management is critical. While both are essential, they serve different purposes and require distinct approaches.

1. **Proactive vs. Reactive**: Risk management is proactive, aiming to prevent or mitigate risks before they become issues. Crisis management is reactive, dealing with events that have already occurred and require immediate attention.
2. **Focus on Prevention vs. Response**: Risk management focuses on identifying and addressing potential risks to prevent crises. Crisis management focuses on responding to and resolving crises to minimize their impact.
3. **Long-Term vs. Short-Term**: Risk management is a continuous, long-term process integrated into business operations and project planning. Crisis management is short-term and situational, activated when a crisis occurs.
4. **Resource Allocation**: Effective risk management can reduce the frequency and severity of crises, leading to more efficient use of resources. Crisis management often requires mobilizing significant resources quickly to address urgent situations.

Example

> ### *Scenario 1: Risk Management*

Situation: A software development company is planning to launch a new product in six months. During the planning phase, the project manager identifies several potential risks, including the possibility of key team members falling ill, unexpected technical challenges, and delays from third-party vendors.

Proactive Measures: The project manager implements the following risk management strategies:

Team Backup Plan: Assigns secondary team members to key roles to cover for any absences.

Technical Challenges: Schedules regular code reviews and allocates extra time for testing and debugging.

Vendor Management: Establishes clear communication channels and backup vendors to mitigate potential delays.

Outcome: By proactively identifying and addressing these risks, the project runs smoothly, and the product is launched on time without major issues. The proactive nature of risk management helped prevent potential crises before they occurred.

Scenario 2: Crisis Management

Situation: A food processing company discovers that one of its products is contaminated with a harmful bacteria, resulting in several consumers falling ill. The news spreads quickly, and the company faces immediate public scrutiny and potential legal action.

Reactive Measures: The crisis management team is activated and takes the following steps:

Immediate Recall: Issues a nationwide recall of the contaminated product to prevent further harm.

> *Public Communication: Releases statements to the media and on social platforms, explaining the situation, apologizing, and detailing the steps being taken to address the issue.*
>
> *Investigation and Resolution: Conducts an internal investigation to determine the source of contamination and implements stricter quality control measures to prevent future incidents.*
>
> *Outcome: The company manages to control the damage by responding quickly and transparently. Although it suffers some reputational harm and financial losses, the prompt and effective crisis management helps restore consumer trust over time.*

All in all..

For business owners and project managers, both risk management and crisis management are indispensable. By proactively managing risks, they can reduce the likelihood of crises and enhance their organization's resilience. When crises do occur, a well-prepared crisis management plan ensures a swift and effective response, minimizing disruption and facilitating recovery. Integrating both approaches into their strategic planning and operational processes enables business owners and project managers to navigate uncertainty and achieve long-term success.

1.4 Key Terms and Definitions

Understanding the terminology associated with risk management is essential for business owners and project managers. These key terms and definitions provide a foundational vocabulary to effectively communicate and implement risk management practices within an organization or project.

1. Risk

Risk is the effect of uncertainty on objectives. It encompasses the potential for both negative and positive outcomes resulting from external and internal factors. In a business context, risks can affect strategic goals, operational efficiency, financial stability, and compliance.

2. Risk Management

Risk management is the process of identifying, assessing, prioritizing, and mitigating risks to minimize their impact on an organization or project. It involves developing strategies to handle potential threats and opportunities, ensuring that objectives are achieved despite uncertainties.

3. Risk Appetite

Risk appetite refers to the level of risk that an organization or project is willing to accept in pursuit of its objectives. It reflects the organization's tolerance for risk and helps guide decision-making processes. Business owners and project managers use risk appetite to balance potential benefits and risks.

4. Risk Assessment

Risk assessment is the systematic process of evaluating the potential risks that could affect an organization or project. It involves analyzing the likelihood and impact of identified risks to prioritize them and determine appropriate mitigation strategies.

5. Risk Identification

Risk identification is the initial step in the risk management process, involving the recognition and documentation of potential risks that could affect an organization or project. Techniques for risk identification include brainstorming, SWOT analysis, expert interviews, and historical data analysis.

6. Risk Mitigation

Risk mitigation involves developing and implementing strategies to reduce the likelihood and/or impact of identified risks. This can include avoiding, transferring, reducing, or accepting risks. Effective risk mitigation helps minimize adverse effects on business objectives or project outcomes.

7. Risk Register

A risk register is a document that records all identified risks, their assessments, and mitigation strategies. It serves as a central repository for tracking and managing risks throughout the risk management process. Business owners and project managers use the risk register to monitor and update risks regularly.

Example:

ID	Risk Description	Category	Likelihood	Impact	Score	Response	Owner	Mitigation Plan	Status
R1	Delays due to key team members falling ill	Operational	Medium	High	12	Mitigation	Project Manager	Assign backup team members to key roles	Open
R2	Critical third-party software component becoming unavailable	Strategic	Medium	High	12	Mitigation	Tech Lead	Identify and evaluate alternative components early	Open
R3	Budget overrun due to underestimating project costs	Financial	Low	High	8	Mitigation	Finance Manager	Conduct detailed cost analysis and add a contingency budget	Open
R4	Non-compliance with updated data protection regulations	Compliance	Low	Medium	6	Transfer	Compliance Officer	Purchase cyber liability insurance	Open
R5	Increase in market demand for a similar product by a competitor	Strategic	High	High	15	Exploitation	Marketing Manager	Accelerate product launch and increase marketing efforts	Open
R6	Server downtime due to hardware failure	Operational	Low	High	8	Mitigation	IT Manager	Implement redundant server infrastructure	Open
R7	Potential partnership opportunity with a major client	Strategic	Medium	High	12	Enhancement	Sales Director	Strengthen proposal and allocate resources to secure partnership	Open
R8	Project scope creep due to additional feature requests	Operational	Medium	Medium	9	Mitigation	Project Manager	Implement a strict change control process	Open
R9	Public backlash due to a controversial feature	Reputational	Low	High	8	Acceptance	PR Manager	Monitor public feedback and prepare a response plan	Open
R10	Delays due to regulatory approval	Compliance	Medium	Medium	9	Mitigation	Regulatory Officer	Engage with regulators early and ensure all documentation is thorough	Open

8. Qualitative Risk Assessment

Qualitative risk assessment involves evaluating risks based on subjective criteria, such as expert judgment and experience. It typically uses descriptive scales (e.g., high, medium, low) to assess the likelihood and impact of risks. This approach is useful for prioritizing risks quickly.

Example:

A construction project team is evaluating the risk of delays due to weather conditions.

Likelihood: Based on expert judgment and historical data, the project team assesses the likelihood of adverse weather conditions as "Medium."

Impact: The team determines that if adverse weather occurs, it would have a "High" impact on the project timeline, causing significant delays.

Risk Rating: Combining these assessments, the overall risk is rated as "High."

This quick, descriptive evaluation allows the team to prioritize weather-related risks and plan mitigation strategies, such as scheduling buffer time and preparing for weatherproofing.

---

9. Quantitative Risk Assessment

Quantitative risk assessment involves evaluating risks using numerical data and statistical methods. Techniques such as Monte Carlo simulation, decision tree analysis, and sensitivity analysis provide more precise estimates of risk likelihood and impact. This approach is useful for detailed risk analysis and decision-making.

Example:

> A software development project is assessing the risk of cost overruns.
>
> Data Collection: The team gathers numerical data on similar past projects, including cost variances and factors contributing to those variances.
>
> Monte Carlo Simulation: They use a Monte Carlo simulation to model the potential cost outcomes based on the collected data. The simulation runs thousands of scenarios, providing a range of possible costs.
>
> Results: The simulation results show that there is a 20% probability that the project will exceed the budget by 15% or more. The expected cost overrun is calculated to be $50,000.
>
> This precise numerical analysis allows the project manager to make informed decisions, such as securing additional funding or adjusting the project scope to stay within budget.

10. Risk Response Planning

Risk response planning involves developing strategies and actions to address identified risks.

The four main types of risk responses for negative risks are:

- **Avoidance**: Eliminating the risk by changing plans or processes.
- **Mitigation**: Reducing the likelihood or impact of the risk.
- **Transfer**: Shifting the risk to a third party, such as through insurance.
- **Acceptance**: Acknowledging the risk and deciding to proceed without additional action.

The four main types of risk responses for positive risks are:

1. **Exploitation**: Taking actions to ensure that the opportunity is realized and benefits are maximized.
2. **Enhancement**: Increasing the likelihood or impact of the opportunity to ensure it is fully realized.
3. **Sharing**: Allocating the opportunity to a third party who is best able to capture the benefits.
4. **Acceptance**: Acknowledging the opportunity and deciding to take advantage of it if it occurs, without proactive action.

Example:

<u>Negative Risk Responses</u>

Avoidance
A company plans to launch a new product, but there is a high risk of failure due to a highly competitive market. To avoid this risk, the company decides to change its plans and focus on improving an existing product line instead of launching a new one.

Mitigation
A construction project faces the risk of delays due to potential bad weather. To mitigate this risk, the project manager implements weather-resistant construction methods and adjusts the project schedule to include buffer time for possible weather-related disruptions.

Transfer
A business is concerned about the risk of financial loss from a data breach. To transfer this risk, the company purchases cyber liability insurance, which will cover the financial impact of a potential breach.

Acceptance
A startup recognizes the risk of early-stage funding running out before achieving profitability. The founders acknowledge this risk but decide to proceed with their current plans, accepting the possibility and preparing to seek additional funding if necessary.

Positive Risk Responses

Exploitation
A tech company identifies an emerging market for a new software application. To exploit this opportunity, the company allocates additional resources to accelerate the development and launch of the software, ensuring it captures the market before competitors.

Enhancement
A consulting firm sees the potential for significant business growth if it can secure a high-profile client. To enhance this opportunity, the firm invests in targeted marketing and strengthens its proposal to increase the likelihood of winning the contract.

Sharing
A pharmaceutical company discovers a promising new drug but lacks the resources to develop it fully. To share this opportunity, the company forms a partnership with a larger pharmaceutical firm, allowing both parties to benefit from the drug's development and commercialization.

Acceptance
A retail company notices a trend that could boost holiday sales. Instead of taking proactive measures, the company decides to continue with its current sales strategy, acknowledging the opportunity and prepared to capitalize on the increased sales if the trend materializes.

11. Contingency Planning

Contingency planning involves preparing for potential risks by developing backup plans and actions. These plans are activated if specific risks materialize, helping to ensure business continuity and minimize disruption.

Example

Scenario: *A retail company relies heavily on its online sales platform. They* recognize that any significant downtime of their website could result in substantial revenue loss, customer dissatisfaction, and damage to their brand reputation. To prepare for this potential risk, they develop a comprehensive contingency plan.

Example of Contingency Planning:

1. **Identified Risk:** Website downtime due to a cyber-attack, server failure, or software glitch.
2. **Backup Plans and Actions:**
    A. Cyber-Attack Contingency Plan:
    - **Risk Assessment:** The company conducts a thorough risk assessment and identifies that a cyber-attack is a significant threat.
    - **Preventive Measures:** Invest in robust cybersecurity measures such as firewalls, intrusion detection systems, regular security audits, and employee training on phishing and other cyber threats.
    - **Incident Response Team:** Form an incident response team with defined roles and responsibilities. This team includes IT security experts, communication specialists, and legal advisors.
    - **Immediate Actions:** If a cyber-attack is detected, the incident response team immediately isolates affected systems to prevent the spread of the attack. They activate backup servers and switch the website to a secure backup environment.
    - **Communication Plan:** Inform customers about the issue through email, social media, and the company's mobile app, assuring them that their data is safe and the website will be fully operational soon.
    - **Recovery and Review:** Once the threat is neutralized, restore normal operations and conduct a post-incident review to improve future contingency plans.
3. **B. Server Failure Contingency Plan:**
    - **Redundancy:** Set up redundant servers in multiple geographic locations to ensure that if one server fails, others can take over with minimal disruption.
    - **Data Backups:** Perform regular data backups and store them securely in multiple locations.

- - **Automatic Failover:** *Implement an automatic failover system that switches traffic to backup servers in case of a primary server failure.*
  - **Technical Support:** *Have a dedicated technical support team available 24/7 to address any server issues immediately.*
4. **C. Software Glitch Contingency Plan:**
    - **Testing and QA:** *Implement rigorous testing and quality assurance processes to minimize the risk of software glitches.*
    - **Rollback Plan:** *Maintain a rollback plan to revert to the previous stable version of the software in case a new update causes issues.*
    - **Customer Support:** *Provide clear instructions and a dedicated customer support line to assist users facing problems due to the software glitch.*

Outcome: *When a cyber-attack occurs, the company's contingency plan is activated. The incident response team isolates the attack, switches to backup servers, and informs customers promptly. As a result, the company experiences minimal downtime, retains customer trust, and quickly resumes normal operations.*

12. Key Risk Indicators (KRIs)

Key Risk Indicators (KRIs) are metrics used to monitor and signal the potential increase in risk exposure. They provide early warning signs of potential issues, enabling business owners and project managers to take proactive measures before risks escalate.

Example

Scenario: *A software development company is working on a critical project with a tight deadline. They want to monitor potential risks to ensure the project stays on track.*

Key Risk Indicator (KRI): Percentage of Code Defects Found During Testing

Explanation: *The company decides to track the percentage of code defects found during each testing phase as a KRI. Here's how this might work:*

1. **Baseline Establishment:** *The company first establishes a baseline for the acceptable percentage of code defects based on historical data from similar projects. For example, they determine that finding 5% of code defects during testing is typical.*
2. **Monitoring:** *During the current project's testing phases (unit testing, integration testing, system testing), the team tracks the percentage of defects found.*
3. **Thresholds and Alerts:** *The company sets thresholds for this KRI. For instance, if the percentage of code defects exceeds 7%, it triggers a yellow alert indicating a moderate risk. If it exceeds 10%, it triggers a red alert indicating a high risk.*
4. **Proactive Measures:** *If a yellow or red alert is triggered, the project manager and team take proactive measures. This might include conducting code reviews, additional testing, or reallocating resources to address the increased defects and prevent further issues.*

Benefits: *By monitoring this KRI, the company gets early warning signs if the quality of the code is deteriorating. This allows them to address potential issues before they escalate, helping to ensure the project stays on track and meets its deadlines.*

Please note this is just one example of a KRI in an IT project. Different industries and projects might have different KRIs based on their specific risk factors and objectives.

13. Enterprise Risk Management (ERM)

Enterprise Risk Management (ERM) is a comprehensive approach to managing all risks across an organization. It integrates risk management into every aspect of the business, aligning it with strategic objectives and ensuring a consistent and coordinated response to risks.

14. Risk Owner

A risk owner is an individual or team responsible for managing a specific risk. This includes implementing mitigation strategies, monitoring the risk, and reporting on its status. Assigning risk owners ensures accountability and effective risk management.

15. Risk Culture

Risk culture refers to the shared values, beliefs, and attitudes towards risk within an organization. A strong risk culture promotes awareness, open communication, and proactive management of risks. Business owners and project managers play a key role in fostering a positive risk culture.

Example

Scenario: *A manufacturing company wants to improve its safety standards and overall approach to risk management. They aim to foster a strong risk culture to ensure the safety of their employees and the reliability of their production processes.*

Example of Risk Culture:

1. **Shared Values and Beliefs:**
   - **Safety First:** *The company adopts the motto "Safety First" and integrates it into every aspect of their operations. This belief is communicated from top management down to every employee, emphasizing that safety is the top priority.*
   - **Continuous Improvement:** *The company believes in continuously improving its processes to minimize risks. This includes regularly reviewing and updating safety protocols and encouraging employees to suggest improvements.*

2. **Attitudes Towards Risk:**
   - **Proactive Risk Management:** *Employees are encouraged to identify potential hazards before they become issues. This proactive approach is supported by regular training sessions on risk identification and management.*
   - **Open Communication:** *The company promotes open communication about risks. Employees feel comfortable reporting safety concerns without fear of retaliation. This attitude is reinforced by management's commitment to addressing reported risks promptly.*
3. **Practices and Actions:**
   - **Regular Safety Audits:** *The company conducts regular safety audits to identify and mitigate risks. These audits are seen as opportunities for improvement rather than punitive measures.*
   - **Risk Management Training:** *All employees, from new hires to senior management, receive ongoing training in risk management practices. This training covers identifying risks, reporting procedures, and emergency response.*
   - **Incentives for Safety:** *The company implements incentive programs to reward employees for exemplary safety practices and proactive risk management. For instance, teams that go the longest without any safety incidents receive recognition and rewards.*
   - **Leadership by Example:** *Business owners and project managers lead by example, consistently following safety protocols and participating in risk management activities. Their behavior reinforces the importance of risk culture throughout the organization.*

16. Scenario Analysis

Scenario analysis involves evaluating the potential impact of different risk scenarios on an organization or project. By exploring various "what-if" situations, business owners and project managers can better understand potential outcomes and develop more robust risk mitigation strategies.

Example:

Scenario: *A logistics company wants to ensure the timely delivery of goods and manage potential risks that could disrupt their supply chain. They conduct a scenario analysis to evaluate the impact of different risk scenarios.*

Example of Scenario Analysis:

1. **Identified Risk Scenarios:**
   - **Scenario 1:** *Natural Disaster*
   - **Scenario 2:** *Supplier Bankruptcy*
   - **Scenario 3:** *Fuel Price Surge*
2. **Evaluating Potential Impacts and Developing Mitigation Strategies:**

   A. Scenario 1: Natural Disaster
   - **Risk Assessment:** *Analyze the likelihood and impact of natural disasters (e.g., hurricanes, earthquakes) affecting key transportation routes and distribution centers.*
   - **Impact Evaluation:**
     - *Disruption in delivery schedules*
     - *Damage to goods in transit*
     - *Increased transportation costs due to rerouting*
   - **Mitigation Strategies:**
     - *Diversify transportation routes and establish alternative routes in advance.*
     - *Partner with multiple carriers to ensure flexibility in logistics.*
     - *Invest in robust packaging solutions to protect goods from potential damage.*
     - *Develop a disaster recovery plan to quickly resume operations.*
3. **B. Scenario 2: Supplier Bankruptcy**
   - **Risk Assessment:** *Assess the financial stability of key*

suppliers and the impact of a major supplier going bankrupt.
- **Impact Evaluation:**
  - Disruption in the supply of critical components or goods
  - Delays in production and delivery schedules
  - Increased costs to find and onboard new suppliers
- **Mitigation Strategies:**
  - Conduct regular financial health checks of key suppliers.
  - Establish relationships with multiple suppliers for critical components.
  - Maintain a buffer stock of essential goods to cover short-term disruptions.
  - Negotiate flexible contracts with suppliers to allow for quick adjustments.

4. **C. Scenario 3: Fuel Price Surge**
   - **Risk Assessment:** Evaluate the potential impact of a significant increase in fuel prices on transportation costs.
   - **Impact Evaluation:**
     - Increased operating costs
     - Higher delivery charges passed on to customers
     - Potential reduction in profit margins
   - **Mitigation Strategies:**
     - Invest in fuel-efficient vehicles and technologies.
     - Explore alternative transportation methods, such as rail or sea, which may be less impacted by fuel price fluctuations.
     - Implement fuel hedging strategies to lock in fuel prices.
     - Optimize delivery routes and schedules to reduce fuel consumption.

5. **Outcome:**
   - **Natural Disaster:** By diversifying transportation routes and establishing alternative carriers, the company can maintain delivery schedules even if a natural disaster occurs. The disaster recovery plan ensures quick resumption of operations.
   - **Supplier Bankruptcy:** Regular financial checks and maintaining relationships with multiple suppliers enable the

> company to switch suppliers quickly, minimizing disruption to the supply chain.
> - **Fuel Price Surge:** Investing in fuel-efficient vehicles and exploring alternative transportation methods help mitigate the impact of fuel price increases on operating costs. Fuel hedging strategies provide cost stability.

17. Risk Tolerance

Risk tolerance is the specific level of risk that an organization or project can withstand without significant negative impact. It is closely related to risk appetite but is more focused on operational limits and thresholds.

18. Risk Communication

Risk communication involves sharing risk-related information with stakeholders. Effective risk communication ensures that all parties understand the risks, their potential impact, and the measures in place to manage them. This transparency builds trust and facilitates collaboration.

19. Risk Governance

Risk governance refers to the policies, procedures, and structures established to oversee and guide risk management activities. It ensures that risk management is integrated into the organization's overall governance framework and aligns with its strategic goals.

20. Risk Management Framework

A risk management framework is a structured approach to managing risks, providing guidelines, processes, and tools for identifying, assessing, and mitigating risks. It ensures a consistent and systematic approach to risk management across the organization or project.

2 FRAMEWORKS AND STANDARDS IN RISK MANAGEMENT

2.1 ISO 31000

Introduction to ISO 31000

ISO 31000 is an international standard for risk management that provides principles, a framework, and a process for managing risk. It aims to help organizations of all sizes and types manage risks effectively to create and protect value. For business owners and project managers, ISO 31000 offers a structured approach to identify, assess, and manage risks, ensuring that their strategies and operations are resilient and sustainable.

Principles of ISO 31000

ISO 31000 is based on the following key principles:

1. **Integrated**: Risk management should be an integral part of all organizational activities.
2. **Structured and Comprehensive**: A structured and comprehensive approach helps achieve consistent and comparable results.
3. **Customized**: The risk management framework and process should be customized to the organization's external and internal context.
4. **Inclusive**: Involvement of stakeholders ensures that risk management considers their knowledge and perspectives.
5. **Dynamic**: Risk management should be responsive to changes in the internal and external environment.
6. **Best Available Information**: Risk management should be based on historical data, experience, stakeholder feedback, observations, forecasts, and expert judgment.
7. **Human and Cultural Factors**: Human behavior and culture significantly influence all aspects of risk management.

8. **Continual Improvement**: Risk management should be continually improved through learning and experience.

Framework for ISO 31000 Implementation

The ISO 31000 framework consists of the following components:

1. **Leadership and Commitment**: Top management should demonstrate leadership and commitment to risk management by integrating it into the organization's governance structure and strategy.
2. **Integration**: Risk management should be integrated into the organization's structure, operations, and processes.
3. **Design**: The design of the risk management framework should be tailored to the organization's context and risk profile.
4. **Implementation**: The risk management framework should be implemented across all levels of the organization.
5. **Evaluation**: The effectiveness of the risk management framework should be regularly evaluated and improved.
6. **Improvement**: Continual improvement should be pursued based on evaluation outcomes and changing circumstances.

Risk Management Process

The risk management process outlined in ISO 31000 includes:

1. **Communication and Consultation**: Engaging with stakeholders to ensure that risk management is based on a comprehensive understanding of the risks.
2. **Scope, Context, and Criteria**: Defining the scope, context, and criteria for risk management activities.
3. **Risk Assessment**: This includes risk identification, risk analysis, and risk evaluation.
4. **Risk Treatment**: Selecting and implementing measures to mitigate or manage risks.

5. **Monitoring and Review**: Continuously monitoring and reviewing the risk management process and risks.
6. **Recording and Reporting**: Documenting and reporting risk management activities and outcomes.

Examples:

Example 1: Manufacturing Business Owner

A manufacturing business owner wants to implement ISO 31000 to enhance risk management in their production process.

1. **Leadership and Commitment**: The owner commits to integrating risk management into the company's strategic planning and operations, appointing a risk management officer to oversee the process.
2. **Integration**: Risk management is embedded into the production planning process. All departments are involved in identifying potential risks, such as supply chain disruptions, equipment failures, and workforce safety issues.
3. **Design**: The risk management framework is customized to the manufacturing context, considering specific risks like machinery breakdown and regulatory compliance.
4. **Implementation**: The company conducts regular risk assessments, identifying critical risks in the production process and developing mitigation strategies, such as maintaining equipment, securing multiple suppliers, and providing safety training.
5. **Evaluation**: The effectiveness of the risk management strategies is evaluated through regular audits and performance reviews.
6. **Improvement**: Based on audit results and feedback, the company continuously improves its risk management practices, updating risk registers and refining mitigation plans.

Example 2: IT Project Manager

An IT project manager is tasked with implementing ISO 31000 to manage risks in a software development project.

1. **Leadership and Commitment**: *The project manager demonstrates commitment by integrating risk management into the project plan and allocating resources for risk management activities.*
2. **Integration**: *Risk management is embedded into the project lifecycle, with risk assessments conducted at each project phase (initiation, planning, execution, and closure).*
3. **Design**: *The risk management framework is tailored to the IT project, focusing on risks such as technical challenges, scope creep, and cybersecurity threats.*
4. **Implementation**: *The project team identifies and analyzes risks during regular risk workshops, developing treatment plans such as adopting agile methodologies, enhancing security protocols, and setting clear project scope boundaries.*
5. **Evaluation**: *The project manager regularly reviews risk management activities during project status meetings, ensuring that risk responses are effective.*
6. **Improvement**: *Lessons learned from each project phase are documented and used to improve risk management practices in future projects.*

All in all…

Implementing ISO 31000 provides a systematic and structured approach to risk management for business owners and project managers. By following its principles, framework, and processes, organizations can enhance their resilience, make informed decisions, and achieve their objectives despite uncertainties. The examples provided illustrate how ISO 31000 can be applied in different contexts, demonstrating its flexibility and value across various industries and projects.

2.2 COSO Framework

Introduction to the COSO Framework

The Committee of Sponsoring Organizations of the Treadway Commission (COSO) framework is a widely recognized model for designing, implementing, and evaluating internal controls and risk management within organizations. It provides a comprehensive approach to managing risks and ensuring that businesses achieve their objectives. For business owners and project managers, the COSO framework offers structured guidelines to enhance their risk management practices, internal controls, and overall governance.

Components of the COSO Framework

The COSO framework consists of five interrelated components:

1. **Control Environment**
2. **Risk Assessment**
3. **Control Activities**
4. **Information and Communication**
5. **Monitoring Activities**

These components are designed to work together to provide an integrated system of internal control and risk management.

1. Control Environment

The control environment sets the tone of the organization, influencing the control consciousness of its people. It includes the integrity, ethical values, and competence of the entity's people; management's philosophy and operating style; the way management assigns authority and responsibility; and the attention and direction provided by the board of directors.

Examples:

> ***Example for Business Owners:***
>
> *A retail business owner establishes a strong control environment by creating a code of conduct, ensuring that ethical behavior is a core value of the company. The owner leads by example, demonstrating integrity and ethical behavior, and ensures that all employees understand and adhere to these values. Additionally, the owner sets clear expectations for performance and accountability, providing regular training and support to staff.*
>
> ***Example for Project Managers:***
>
> *A project manager in a construction company fosters a positive control environment by setting clear ethical guidelines and expectations for the project team. The project manager regularly communicates the importance of compliance and integrity, ensuring that team members understand their roles and responsibilities. The project manager also promotes a culture of accountability, where team members feel empowered to report issues or concerns without fear of retaliation.*

2. Risk Assessment

Risk assessment involves identifying and analyzing risks to achieving the entity's objectives, forming a basis for determining how the risks should be managed. It includes assessing the likelihood and impact of risks and considering how they should be mitigated.

Example:

> **Example for Business Owners:**
>
> *A manufacturing business owner conducts regular risk assessments to identify potential threats to production, such as supply chain disruptions, equipment failures, and regulatory changes. The owner evaluates the likelihood and impact of these risks, prioritizing them based on their potential effect on business objectives. Based on the assessment, the owner develops mitigation strategies, such as diversifying suppliers, investing in preventive maintenance, and staying updated on regulatory requirements.*
>
> **Example for Project Managers:**
>
> *An IT project manager performs a risk assessment at the start of a software development project, identifying risks such as technical challenges, scope creep, and resource constraints. The project manager analyzes these risks to determine their likelihood and potential impact on the project's success. The manager then develops risk response plans, such as implementing agile methodologies, clearly defining project scope, and ensuring adequate resource allocation.*

3. Control Activities

Control activities are the actions taken to address risks and achieve objectives. They include policies and procedures that help ensure management directives are carried out and necessary actions are taken to address risks.

Example:

> **Example for Business Owners:**

A business owner of a financial services firm implements control activities such as segregation of duties, regular reconciliations, and authorization requirements for transactions. These controls help ensure that no single employee has control over all aspects of any financial transaction, reducing the risk of fraud and errors. The owner also establishes procedures for regular internal audits to verify compliance with policies.

Example for Project Managers:

A project manager in the construction industry establishes control activities to ensure project quality and safety. These include regular site inspections, quality control checks, and adherence to safety protocols. The project manager also implements change management procedures to control scope changes, ensuring that any modifications to the project plan are properly reviewed and approved.

4. Information and Communication

Information and communication involve identifying, capturing, and communicating relevant information in a form and timeframe that enable people to carry out their responsibilities. It includes both internal and external communication.

Example:

Example for Business Owners:

A business owner in the hospitality industry ensures effective information and communication by implementing a centralized information system that captures data on bookings, guest preferences, and feedback. The owner communicates key information regularly through staff meetings, newsletters, and an internal portal. This ensures that employees are informed about business performance, customer feedback, and any changes in procedures.

Example for Project Managers:

A project manager in a marketing agency establishes clear communication channels for the project team, including regular status meetings, project dashboards, and collaborative tools like project management software. The project manager ensures that all team members and stakeholders are kept informed about project progress, risks, and changes, facilitating transparency and effective decision-making.

5. Monitoring Activities

Monitoring activities involve ongoing evaluations to assess the effectiveness of internal control and risk management systems. It includes regular management and supervisory activities, as well as separate evaluations such as internal audits.

Example:

Example for Business Owners:

A business owner of a healthcare clinic implements monitoring activities by conducting regular performance reviews and audits of clinical practices and administrative processes. The owner also establishes key performance indicators (KPIs) to track patient satisfaction, operational efficiency, and compliance with healthcare regulations. These monitoring activities help the owner identify areas for improvement and ensure continuous compliance with standards.

> *Example for Project Managers:*
>
> *A project manager in the construction sector sets up monitoring activities by scheduling regular project reviews and progress assessments. The project manager uses project management software to track milestones, budgets, and resource allocation. Additionally, the project manager conducts post-project evaluations to capture lessons learned and improve future project performance.*

All in all..

The COSO framework provides a comprehensive and flexible approach to managing risks and ensuring effective internal controls. For business owners and project managers, implementing COSO's components helps create a robust risk management culture, enhances operational efficiency, and ensures the achievement of strategic objectives. The examples provided illustrate how the COSO framework can be applied in different contexts, demonstrating its versatility and value across various industries and projects.

2.3 PMBOK GUIDE ON RISK MANAGEMENT

Introduction to the PMBOK Guide

The Project Management Body of Knowledge (PMBOK) Guide, published by the Project Management Institute (PMI), is a widely recognized standard for project management. It provides a comprehensive framework for managing projects, including a detailed approach to risk management. For business owners and project managers, the PMBOK Guide offers valuable insights and methodologies to identify, analyze, and respond to project risks effectively.

Risk Management Process Groups

The PMBOK Guide outlines six primary processes for risk management within the project management framework:

1. **Plan Risk Management**
2. **Identify Risks**
3. **Perform Qualitative Risk Analysis**
4. **Perform Quantitative Risk Analysis**
5. **Plan Risk Responses**
6. **Monitor Risks**

1. Plan Risk Management

This process involves defining how to conduct risk management activities for a project. It ensures that the level, type, and visibility of risk management are proportionate to both the risks and the importance of the project to the organization.

Key Activities:

- **Defining risk management roles and responsibilities**: Assigning team members specific tasks related to risk management.
- **Establishing risk management processes and templates**: Creating standard forms and procedures to ensure consistency.
- **Setting risk thresholds and criteria**: Determining acceptable levels of risk for the project.

Examples

Example for Business Owners:

A business owner planning to launch a new product line defines a risk management plan that includes identifying potential market risks, assigning responsibilities for monitoring these risks to the marketing team, and establishing criteria for acceptable risk levels based on market research and historical data.

Example for Project Managers:

A project manager in a software development project develops a risk management plan outlining the risk identification process, assigning roles to team members for monitoring specific technical risks, and setting risk thresholds based on project milestones and deliverables.

2. Identify Risks

This process involves determining which risks might affect the project and documenting their characteristics. It includes gathering input from stakeholders and using various techniques to uncover potential risks.

Key Activities:

- **Brainstorming sessions**: Engaging project team members and stakeholders to identify possible risks.
- **SWOT analysis**: Analyzing the project's strengths, weaknesses, opportunities, and threats.
- **Expert interviews**: Consulting with experts to gain insights into potential risks.

Examples

Example for Business Owners:

A retail business owner conducts a SWOT analysis with the management team to identify potential risks associated with opening a new store, such as competition, location challenges, and supply chain disruptions. The risks are documented and categorized for further analysis.

Example for Project Managers:

A construction project manager holds brainstorming sessions with the project team and stakeholders to identify risks related to site conditions, regulatory approvals, and subcontractor performance. The identified risks are recorded in a risk register for ongoing monitoring and management.

3. Perform Qualitative Risk Analysis

This process involves prioritizing risks for further analysis or action by assessing their probability of occurrence and impact. It helps to focus on high-priority risks and allocate resources effectively.

Key Activities:

- **Risk probability and impact assessment**: Evaluating the likelihood and consequences of each identified risk.
- **Risk categorization**: Grouping risks by sources, such as technical, external, organizational, or project management.
- **Risk urgency assessment**: Determining the timeframe within which risks need to be addressed.

Examples

Example for Business Owners:

A business owner prioritizes identified risks for a new marketing campaign by assessing the probability of each risk occurring and its potential impact on campaign success. High-priority risks, such as regulatory changes and customer feedback, are flagged for immediate attention.

Example for Project Managers:

An IT project manager performs qualitative risk analysis for a system upgrade project, evaluating the probability and impact of risks like data migration errors and user resistance. The highest-priority risks are categorized and assigned to team members for detailed analysis and response planning.

4. Perform Quantitative Risk Analysis

This process involves numerically analyzing the effect of identified risks on overall project objectives. It provides a quantitative approach to decision-making, helping to understand the potential impact of risks on project outcomes.

Key Activities:

- **Monte Carlo simulation**: Using statistical techniques to model the impact of risks on project schedules and costs.
- **Decision tree analysis**: Evaluating decision options and their associated risks and rewards.
- **Sensitivity analysis**: Determining which risks have the most significant impact on project objectives.

Examples

Example for Business Owners:

A business owner uses Monte Carlo simulation to analyze the potential financial impact of risks associated with a new investment. This quantitative

> *analysis helps in making informed decisions about risk mitigation strategies and contingency planning.*
>
> ***Example for Project Managers:***
>
> *A project manager for a large infrastructure project performs quantitative risk analysis using decision tree analysis to evaluate the potential outcomes of different risk response strategies, such as additional funding or schedule adjustments. This helps in selecting the most cost-effective and impactful risk responses.*

5. Plan Risk Responses

This process involves developing options and actions to enhance opportunities and reduce threats to project objectives. It includes selecting the most appropriate response strategies for identified risks.

Key Activities:

- **Avoidance**: Changing the project plan to eliminate the risk.
- **Mitigation**: Reducing the probability or impact of the risk.
- **Transfer**: Shifting the risk to a third party, such as through insurance or outsourcing.
- **Acceptance**: Acknowledging the risk and deciding to deal with its consequences if it occurs.

Examples

> ***Example for Business Owners:***
>
> *A business owner planning an international expansion develops risk response strategies, such as purchasing insurance to transfer financial risks*

and establishing partnerships to mitigate risks related to market entry and local regulations.

Example for Project Managers:

A project manager for a renewable energy project plans risk responses for potential technical failures by implementing mitigation strategies like additional testing and quality control measures. Risks that cannot be mitigated are accepted with contingency plans in place.

For a detailed example of each Risk Response strategy please check *Chapter 1.4 Key Terms and Definitions* section 10. Risk Response Planning

6. Monitor Risks

This process involves tracking identified risks, monitoring residual risks, identifying new risks, and evaluating the effectiveness of risk response strategies. It ensures that risk management remains an ongoing activity throughout the project lifecycle.

Key Activities:

- **Regular risk reviews**: Conducting periodic assessments of the risk register and response plans.
- **Risk audits**: Evaluating the effectiveness of risk management processes and controls.
- **Status reporting**: Keeping stakeholders informed about the current risk status and any changes.

Example for Business Owners:

A business owner regularly reviews the risk register for a new product launch, monitoring the effectiveness of risk response strategies and updating the register with any new risks identified during the process. Regular reports are shared with the management team to ensure ongoing awareness and action.

Example for Project Managers:

A project manager for an IT implementation project conducts monthly risk reviews, assessing the status of identified risks and the effectiveness of implemented responses. New risks are added to the risk register, and the project team is updated on the current risk landscape and any necessary adjustments to risk management plans.

Conclusion

The PMBOK Guide provides a systematic and structured approach to risk management that helps business owners and project managers effectively identify, analyze, and respond to risks. By following the processes outlined in the PMBOK Guide, organizations can enhance their ability to manage uncertainties and achieve project success. The examples provided demonstrate how the PMBOK risk management processes can be applied in various contexts, highlighting their practical value for different industries and projects.

2.4 INDUSTRY-SPECIFIC STANDARDS

In addition to general risk management frameworks such as ISO 31000 and the COSO framework, many industries have developed specific standards to address the unique risks and regulatory requirements they face. We do not expect you to read them all; rather, we encourage you to jump directly to the ones related to your areas of interest. These industry-specific standards provide detailed guidelines and best practices to help organizations manage risks effectively within their specific contexts.

1. Financial Services

- **Basel III**: International regulatory framework for banks, focusing on risk management and bank capital adequacy.
- **ISO 22301**: Business continuity management systems – Requirements.
- **COSO ERM Framework**: Enterprise Risk Management – Integrating with Strategy and Performance.
- **Solvency II**: Regulatory framework for the insurance industry in the European Union, focusing on capital adequacy and risk management.

2. Healthcare

- **ISO 14971**: Application of risk management to medical devices.
- **HIPAA (Health Insurance Portability and Accountability Act)**: U.S. standard for protecting sensitive patient data.
- **JCAHO (Joint Commission on Accreditation of Healthcare Organizations)**: Standards for patient safety and quality of care in healthcare organizations.
- **FDA (Food and Drug Administration) Regulations**: Various regulations focusing on risk management for pharmaceuticals, medical devices, and other healthcare products.

3. Information Technology

- **ISO/IEC 27001**: Information security management systems – Requirements.
- **NIST SP 800-37**: Risk Management Framework for Information Systems and Organizations.
- **COBIT (Control Objectives for Information and Related Technologies)**: Framework for developing, implementing, monitoring, and improving IT governance and management practices.
- **ITIL (Information Technology Infrastructure Library)**: Framework for IT service management focusing on aligning IT services with business needs.

4. Manufacturing

- **ISO 9001**: Quality management systems – Requirements.
- **ISO 31010**: Risk management – Risk assessment techniques.
- **IEC 61508**: Functional safety of electrical/electronic/programmable electronic safety-related systems.
- **ISO 45001**: Occupational health and safety management systems – Requirements with guidance for use.

5. Energy and Utilities

- **ISO 55001**: Asset management – Management systems – Requirements.
- **IEC 31010**: Risk management – Risk assessment techniques.
- **API RP 580**: Risk-based inspection.
- **NERC (North American Electric Reliability Corporation) Standards**: Various standards focusing on the reliability and security of the North American bulk power system.

6. Construction

- **ISO 31000**: Risk management – Guidelines.
- **PMI PMBOK (Project Management Body of Knowledge) Guide**: Standards for project risk management.
- **CII (Construction Industry Institute) Best Practices**: Risk management best practices for the construction industry.
- **FIDIC (International Federation of Consulting Engineers) Contracts**: Standard forms of contract and guidelines that include risk management clauses.

7. Aerospace and Defense

- **AS9100**: Quality management systems – Requirements for aviation, space, and defense organizations.
- **MIL-STD-882**: Standard practice for system safety in the defense industry.
- **DO-178C/ED-12C**: Software considerations in airborne systems and equipment certification.

- **ISO 27002**: Code of practice for information security controls.

8. Telecommunications

- **ISO/IEC 27011**: Information security management guidelines for telecommunications organizations.
- **ITU-T X.1055**: Risk management framework for information security in telecommunications.
- **ETSI (European Telecommunications Standards Institute) EN 319 401**: General policy requirements for trust service providers.

9. Food and Beverage

- **ISO 22000**: Food safety management systems – Requirements for any organization in the food chain.
- **HACCP (Hazard Analysis and Critical Control Points)**: Management system addressing food safety through the analysis and control of biological, chemical, and physical hazards.
- **GFSI (Global Food Safety Initiative)**: Benchmarking standards for food safety management systems.
- **BRC (British Retail Consortium) Global Standards**: Global standards for food safety, packaging, and other consumer products.

10. Transportation and Logistics

- **ISO 28000**: Specification for security management systems for the supply chain.
- **IATA Operational Safety Audit (IOSA)**: Global airline operational safety and management standards.
- **IMO (International Maritime Organization) ISM Code**: International Safety Management Code for the safe operation of ships and pollution prevention.
- **TAPA (Transported Asset Protection Association) Standards**: Security standards for logistics and supply chain operations.

11. Public Sector and Government

- **ISO 37001**: Anti-bribery management systems – Requirements with guidance for use.
- **COSO ERM Framework**: Enterprise Risk Management – Integrating with Strategy and Performance.
- **OCEG (Open Compliance and Ethics Group) GRC Capability Model**: Framework for governance, risk management, and compliance.
- **GAO (Government Accountability Office) Standards**: Standards for internal control in the federal government.

All in all…

Industry-specific standards provide tailored guidelines and best practices to address the unique risks and regulatory requirements of various sectors. By adopting these standards, organizations can enhance their risk management capabilities, ensure compliance with industry regulations, and improve overall operational resilience. This comprehensive list covers a wide range of industries, illustrating the breadth and depth of risk management standards available to business owners and project managers.

3 RISK IDENTIFICATION

3.1 TECHNIQUES FOR IDENTIFYING RISKS

Effective risk management begins with identifying potential risks that may impact the achievement of project objectives or business goals. Various techniques can be employed to systematically uncover risks and ensure comprehensive coverage. Each technique offers unique advantages in terms of depth of analysis, stakeholder involvement, and applicability to different types of risks.

3.1.1 BRAINSTORMING

Description: Brainstorming is a group creativity technique used to generate a large number of ideas or solutions to a problem. In the context of risk management, it involves a structured session where project team members and stakeholders gather to identify as many potential risks as possible.

Process:

- **Preparation**: Define the scope and objectives of the brainstorming session. Invite relevant stakeholders, including subject matter experts (SMEs) and key project team members.
- **Session Facilitation**: A facilitator guides the brainstorming session, encouraging participants to freely contribute ideas without criticism. Participants are prompted to think broadly about potential risks across various aspects of the project.
- **Idea Generation**: Participants generate ideas by answering questions such as "What could go wrong?" or "What external factors might impact our project?"
- **Documentation**: Capture all identified risks on a whiteboard, flip chart, or digital tool. Each risk should be documented succinctly to preserve its essence and relevance.

Benefits:

- **Diverse Perspectives**: Involves multiple stakeholders with diverse backgrounds and expertise.
- **Creativity**: Encourages out-of-the-box thinking to uncover unconventional risks.
- **Team Building**: Fosters collaboration and engagement among team members.

Considerations:

- **Time-Boxing**: Limit the duration of the session to maintain focus and productivity.
- **Facilitation Skills**: A skilled facilitator is essential to ensure active participation and manage group dynamics.
- **Follow-Up**: Validate and prioritize identified risks after the session to determine their significance and develop appropriate responses.

Example

> *During a brainstorming session for a software development project, team members identified potential risks such as scope creep due to changing client requirements, integration challenges with existing systems, and delays in third-party vendor deliverables.*

3.1.2 Delphi Technique

Description: The Delphi technique is a structured communication method designed to reach consensus among a panel of experts on a particular issue or topic, such as identifying and prioritizing project risks.

Process:

- **Panel Selection**: Identify a panel of experts who possess relevant knowledge and experience in the project domain.

- **Anonymous Feedback**: Distribute a series of questionnaires or surveys to panel members anonymously. Each round of feedback includes questions about potential risks and their likelihood and impact.
- **Iterative Process**: Collate responses from each round, summarize key findings, and provide anonymized feedback to participants in subsequent rounds.
- **Consensus Building**: Through multiple rounds of feedback and controlled communication, aim to achieve convergence on the most critical risks.

Benefits:

- **Expertise Utilization**: Draws upon the insights and expertise of knowledgeable individuals.
- **Anonymity**: Reduces bias and groupthink, allowing for independent thought and opinion sharing.
- **Iterative Refinement**: Facilitates progressive refinement of risk identification based on ongoing feedback.

Considerations:

- **Resource Intensive**: Requires coordination and time to conduct multiple rounds of feedback.
- **Panel Composition**: Selecting appropriate experts with diverse perspectives and avoiding potential conflicts of interest.
- **Data Analysis**: Requires systematic analysis and synthesis of qualitative data from multiple rounds of responses.

Example

> *In a Delphi study involving cybersecurity experts, consensus was reached on high-priority risks such as data breaches due to inadequate encryption*

> *protocols, insider threats from disgruntled employees, and vulnerabilities in third-party software integrations.*

3.1.3 SWOT Analysis

Description: SWOT (Strengths, Weaknesses, Opportunities, Threats) analysis is a strategic planning tool used to identify and evaluate the internal strengths and weaknesses of an organization, as well as external opportunities and threats.

Process:

- **Internal Assessment (Strengths and Weaknesses)**: Identify strengths and weaknesses within the organization that could impact project objectives or contribute to risk exposure.
- **External Assessment (Opportunities and Threats)**: Evaluate external factors such as market conditions, regulatory changes, competitive landscape, and economic trends that could pose risks to the project.

Benefits:

- **Holistic View**: Considers both internal and external factors influencing project risks.
- **Strategic Alignment**: Helps align risk management efforts with broader organizational strategies.
- **Simplicity**: Easy to understand and implement, making it accessible to a wide range of stakeholders.

Considerations:

- **Subjectivity**: Interpretation of SWOT factors may vary among stakeholders.
- **Focus**: May not capture all detailed risks compared to other more specific techniques.

- **Integration**: Ensure findings from SWOT analysis are integrated into the broader risk management plan.

Example

> *A SWOT analysis for a startup company identified opportunities in emerging markets and technological advancements, while also highlighting threats such as intense competition from established firms and regulatory changes affecting product launch timelines.*

3.1.4 EXPERT INTERVIEWS

Description: Expert interviews involve engaging individuals with specialized knowledge or experience relevant to the project or industry to identify and assess potential risks.

Process:

- **Identify Experts**: Select individuals who possess deep knowledge and experience related to specific areas of the project or industry.
- **Structured Interviews**: Conduct one-on-one or group interviews with selected experts using a predefined set of questions focused on identifying risks.
- **Probe for Details**: Ask follow-up questions to explore nuances and underlying factors that could contribute to risk exposure.
- **Document Findings**: Capture insights, perspectives, and identified risks from expert interviews for further analysis and integration into the risk management plan.

Benefits:

- **In-Depth Insights**: Tap into specialized knowledge that may not be readily available within the project team.

- **Contextual Understanding**: Gain a deeper understanding of complex or industry-specific risks.
- **Validation**: Provides validation of identified risks through expert opinion and experience.

Considerations:

- **Resource Requirements**: Requires time and effort to coordinate and conduct interviews with experts.
- **Selection Criteria**: Ensure experts selected represent diverse viewpoints and relevant expertise.
- **Data Integration**: Synthesize findings from multiple interviews to identify common themes and prioritize risks effectively.

Example

> *In an expert interview with a cybersecurity consultant, critical risks such as ransomware attacks targeting sensitive customer data, vulnerabilities in network infrastructure, and gaps in employee cybersecurity training were identified as significant threats to a financial services firm.*

3.2 COMMON SOURCES OF RISK

Identifying common sources of risk is crucial for business owners and project managers to effectively anticipate and manage potential threats that could impact project success or business operations. These sources of risk can arise from various aspects of the internal and external environment, necessitating proactive mitigation strategies to minimize their impact.

1. Internal Sources of Risk

a. Organizational Changes: Changes in leadership, organizational structure, or business processes can introduce uncertainty and resistance, affecting project timelines and stakeholder alignment.

b. Resource Constraints: Limited budget, staffing shortages, or insufficient technological capabilities may hinder project execution and lead to delays or quality issues.

c. Scope Creep: Poorly defined project scope or frequent changes in requirements can result in scope creep, causing budget overruns and timeline extensions.

d. Inadequate Planning: Insufficient planning, including unrealistic schedules, inadequate risk assessment, or unclear objectives, increases the likelihood of project failure or suboptimal outcomes.

2. External Sources of Risk

a. Market Conditions: Fluctuations in market demand, economic downturns, or changes in consumer behavior can impact revenue streams and project viability.

b. Regulatory Changes: Amendments to industry regulations, compliance requirements, or legal obligations may necessitate costly adjustments and operational disruptions.

c. Supplier or Vendor Risks: Dependency on external suppliers or vendors for critical resources or services exposes businesses to supply chain disruptions, delivery delays, or quality issues.

d. Technological Changes: Rapid advancements in technology, cybersecurity threats, or infrastructure failures pose risks to data integrity, operational continuity, and customer trust.

3. Environmental Sources of Risk

a. Natural Disasters: Events such as earthquakes, hurricanes, or floods can disrupt operations, damage infrastructure, and impact supply chains, requiring contingency planning and disaster recovery strategies.

b. Geopolitical Factors: Political instability, trade conflicts, or international sanctions may affect market access, currency exchange rates, and global supply chain logistics.

c. Climate Change: Environmental sustainability concerns, regulatory pressures, and physical risks from climate-related events pose challenges to business operations and long-term planning.

d. Pandemics and Health Crises: Public health emergencies, such as pandemics or outbreaks, can disrupt workforce availability, supply chains, and customer demand, emphasizing the need for robust business continuity plans.

Role of Business Owners and Project Managers:

- **Risk Awareness and Assessment:** Business owners and project managers must continuously assess and prioritize risks, considering their potential impact on strategic objectives and operational performance.
- **Mitigation and Response Planning:** For example, consider a project manager overseeing the construction of a new office building. They identify a risk of potential delays due to a shortage of skilled labor in the local market. To mitigate this, the project manager develops a contingency plan to recruit additional contractors from neighboring cities and implements cross-training programs to upskill existing team members.
- **Stakeholder Communication:** Effectively communicate risks and mitigation strategies to stakeholders, fostering transparency and alignment across teams and external partners.

- **Continuous Improvement:** Foster a culture of continuous improvement by learning from past experiences, adapting risk management strategies to evolving circumstances, and integrating lessons learned into future projects and business operations.

All in all…

By systematically addressing common sources of risk and applying proactive risk management strategies, business owners and project managers can enhance resilience, optimize resource allocation, and maintain a competitive advantage in dynamic and uncertain business environments.

3.3 RISK REGISTER DEVELOPMENT

A risk register is a vital tool in risk management that systematically captures, prioritizes, and tracks potential risks throughout the project lifecycle. It serves as a central repository of information, enabling project managers and business owners to effectively identify, assess, and manage risks to achieve project objectives and organizational goals.

Role of Project Managers and Business Owners:

Both project managers and business owners play crucial roles in the development and utilization of a risk register:

- **Project Manager:** Responsible for overseeing the day-to-day operations of the project, the project manager takes the lead in identifying risks, assessing their impact and likelihood, developing response strategies, and monitoring risk mitigation activities. They ensure that the risk register is regularly updated and that risk management practices align with project timelines and objectives.
- **Business Owner:** As stakeholders with a vested interest in project outcomes and organizational success, business owners provide strategic direction and support for risk management efforts. They approve risk management plans, provide resources and support for risk mitigation activities, and review the risk register to understand

the overall risk exposure and its potential impact on business objectives.

Content of a Risk Register:

We briefly introduced the risk register earlier in the book, let's now jump into specifics. A comprehensive risk register typically includes the following key information for each identified risk:

1. **Risk ID:** A unique identifier assigned to each risk for easy reference and tracking.
2. **Risk Description:** A clear and concise description of the risk, including its potential impact on project objectives or business outcomes.
3. **Risk Category:** Categorization of the risk based on its nature (e.g., technical, financial, organizational) to facilitate targeted risk management strategies.
4. **Risk Owner:** The individual or team responsible for overseeing the management of the risk, including implementing response actions and monitoring its status.
5. **Likelihood:** An assessment of the probability or frequency with which the risk event may occur (e.g., low, medium, high).
6. **Impact:** An evaluation of the potential consequences or severity of the risk event if it were to occur (e.g., low, medium, high).
7. **Risk Response Strategy:** The planned approach for addressing the risk, such as mitigation (reduce likelihood or impact), avoidance (eliminate the risk), transfer (assign to a third party), or acceptance (tolerate the risk).
8. **Mitigation Actions:** Specific actions or measures taken to reduce the likelihood or impact of the risk, including timelines, responsible parties, and progress tracking.
9. **Contingency Plans:** Predefined actions to be implemented if the risk event materializes despite mitigation efforts, ensuring continuity and minimizing disruptions.

10. **Status and Updates:** Regular updates on the status of each risk, including changes in likelihood, impact, response strategies, and mitigation actions.

Example

Risk identified in a Risk Register:

- ***Risk ID:*** *R001*
- ***Risk Description:*** *Potential delay in delivery of critical project components due to supplier issues.*
- ***Risk Category:*** *Supply Chain*
- ***Risk Owner:*** *Project Manager*
- ***Likelihood:*** *Medium*
- ***Impact:*** *High*
- ***Risk Response Strategy:*** *Mitigation (Identify alternative suppliers, negotiate backup contracts)*
- ***Mitigation Actions:*** *Conduct supplier assessments, develop contingency plans, monitor supplier performance monthly.*
- ***Contingency Plans:*** *Expedite shipping, reallocate resources to other project areas.*

Note that a Risk Register is usually presented in a table format. Please check [Chapter 1.4 Key Terms and Definitions](#) section 7. Risk register

4 Risk Assessment

4.1 Qualitative Risk Assessment

Qualitative risk assessment is a critical step in the risk management process, providing a systematic approach to evaluate and prioritize risks based on their characteristics and potential impact on project objectives or business goals. This method relies on subjective judgment and expert opinion rather than quantitative measures, making it accessible and practical for a wide range of projects and business contexts.

Role of Project Managers and Business Owners:

- **Project Managers:** Responsible for facilitating the qualitative risk assessment process within the project team, ensuring all relevant risks are identified, described, and evaluated. Project managers use their expertise to guide discussions, encourage input from all stakeholders, and document the results.
- **Business Owners:** Provide strategic oversight and input during the assessment process, ensuring that the identified risks align with broader business objectives and priorities. Business owners review the assessment outcomes, offer their insights, and endorse the prioritization of risks for further action.

Steps in Qualitative Risk Assessment:

1. **Risk Identification:** The first step involves gathering a comprehensive list of potential risks that could impact the project or business. This can be done through brainstorming sessions, expert interviews, and other techniques discussed in earlier sections.
2. **Risk Description:** Clearly describe each identified risk, including its potential cause, the event itself, and its possible consequences. A well-defined risk description ensures all stakeholders have a common understanding of the risk.
3. **Likelihood Assessment:** Evaluate the probability of each risk occurring. This assessment is often based on expert judgment,

historical data, and the context of the project or business. Likelihood is typically rated on a scale such as Low, Medium, or High.
4. **Impact Assessment:** Determine the potential consequences of each risk if it were to materialize. Consider factors such as cost, time, scope, and quality for projects, or financial performance, operational disruption, and reputational damage for businesses. Impact is usually rated on a similar scale: Low, Medium, or High.
5. **Risk Matrix Development:** Use a risk matrix to plot the likelihood and impact of each risk. This visual tool helps prioritize risks by showing which ones have the highest potential to affect the project or business. Risks in the high-likelihood/high-impact quadrant require immediate attention.
6. **Risk Ranking and Prioritization:** Based on the matrix, rank the risks in order of priority. Focus resources and mitigation efforts on the most significant risks first. This prioritization helps ensure that critical risks are addressed proactively.
7. **Documentation and Communication:** Document the findings of the qualitative risk assessment in a risk register. Ensure all relevant stakeholders, including project team members and business owners, are informed about the risks and their prioritization. Regular communication fosters transparency and alignment.

Example

Consider a project to launch a new software product:

1. **Risk Identification:** *Potential risks include delays in software development, budget overruns, and cybersecurity threats.*
2. **Risk Description:** *A cybersecurity threat might be described as "Potential vulnerability in the software code leading to unauthorized access and data breaches."*
3. **Likelihood Assessment:** *The likelihood of this risk occurring is assessed as Medium, based on the complexity of the software and previous experiences.*

4. **Impact Assessment:** *The impact is rated as High due to potential legal penalties, loss of customer trust, and financial losses.*
5. **Risk Matrix Development:** *The cybersecurity threat is placed in the Medium-Likelihood/High-Impact quadrant.*
6. **Risk Ranking and Prioritization:** *This risk is prioritized highly, warranting immediate mitigation efforts such as code reviews and security audits.*
7. **Documentation and Communication:** *The risk and its assessment are recorded in the risk register, and all stakeholders are informed about the identified risk and planned mitigation actions.*

Benefits of Qualitative Risk Assessment:

- **Efficiency:** Allows for rapid assessment and prioritization of risks without requiring extensive data or complex calculations.
- **Stakeholder Involvement:** Engages project team members and business owners in the risk assessment process, fostering collaboration and shared understanding.
- **Flexibility:** Adaptable to different types of projects and business contexts, making it a versatile tool for risk management.

All in all...

By conducting qualitative risk assessments, project managers and business owners can proactively identify and address risks, enhancing the likelihood of project success and achieving business objectives. This process ensures that resources are focused on the most critical risks, thereby minimizing potential disruptions and maximizing positive outcomes.

4.2 Quantitative Risk Assessment

Quantitative risk assessment involves numerically analyzing the effects of identified risks on project objectives or business goals. This method uses statistical and mathematical models to quantify the probability and impact of risks, providing a more objective basis for decision-making. It helps project managers and business owners to better understand potential outcomes and to plan accordingly.

Role of Project Managers and Business Owners:

- **Project Managers:** Utilize quantitative methods to analyze risks, develop mitigation strategies, and optimize project plans. They leverage data to provide accurate forecasts and scenarios, ensuring project objectives are met within budget and on schedule.
- **Business Owners:** Rely on quantitative risk assessments to make informed strategic decisions, allocate resources efficiently, and maximize returns on investments. They use the insights gained to steer the business towards sustainable growth and resilience.

Example

Scenario: A construction company is planning to build a new office complex. They want to perform a quantitative risk assessment to analyze the effects of identified risks on the project timeline and budget.

Example of Quantitative Risk Assessment:

1. **Identified Risks:**
    - **Risk 1: Delays due to weather conditions**
    - **Risk 2: Increase in material costs**
    - **Risk 3: Labor shortages**
2. **Quantitative Analysis:**
    - **Risk 1: Delays due to weather conditions**
        - **Probability:** *Historical weather data suggests a 20% chance of severe weather causing delays.*

- **Impact:** *If delays occur, they could extend the project timeline by up to 15 days, costing an additional $50,000 in labor and equipment rental.*
- **Expected Value Calculation:** *Expected Value=Probability×Impact=0.20×$50,000=$10,000*
  - **Risk 2: Increase in material costs**
    - **Probability:** *Market analysis indicates a 30% chance of material costs increasing by 10%.*
    - **Impact:** *If material costs rise, the total increase in expenses could be $100,000.*
    - **Expected Value Calculation:** *Expected Value=Probability×Impact=0.30×$100,000=$30,000*
  - **Risk 3: Labor shortages**
    - **Probability:** *Industry reports show a 25% likelihood of labor shortages.*
    - **Impact:** *Labor shortages could delay the project by 20 days, resulting in additional costs of $80,000.*
    - **Expected Value Calculation:** *Expected Value=Probability×Impact=0.25×$80,000=$20,000*
  - **Sum of Expected Values:** *The total potential financial impact of the identified risks is the sum of the expected values:*

  Total Expected Value=$10,000+$30,000+$20,000=$60,000

3. **Decision-Making:**
   - **Risk Mitigation Plans:**
     - **Weather Delays:** *Invest in advanced weather forecasting tools and develop a contingency plan for rescheduling work during severe weather.*
     - **Material Costs:** *Lock in prices with suppliers through long-term contracts to hedge against price increases.*
     - **Labor Shortages:** *Establish partnerships with labor agencies to ensure a steady supply of skilled workers.*
4. **Outcome:**
   - *The construction company uses the quantitative risk assessment to allocate a risk contingency budget of $60,000. They also implement the identified mitigation strategies to minimize the impact of these risks on the project timeline*

> *and budget.*

4.2.1 MONTE CARLO SIMULATION

Monte Carlo Simulation is a powerful quantitative technique that uses random sampling and statistical modeling to estimate the probability distributions of potential outcomes. It helps in understanding the impact of risk and uncertainty on project schedules, costs, and performance.

Example

Consider a project to develop a new product. The project manager identifies uncertainties in the development time and cost. Using Monte Carlo Simulation, they can create a model that includes these uncertainties and simulate thousands of scenarios. This provides a probability distribution of possible project completion dates and costs.

Steps:

1. **Identify Variables:** Determine the key variables affecting the project, such as development time and cost.
2. **Assign Probability Distributions:** Assign probability distributions to these variables based on historical data and expert judgment.
3. **Run Simulations:** Use software to run thousands of simulations, each time randomly selecting values for the variables from their assigned distributions.
4. **Analyze Results:** Analyze the results to determine the probability of meeting project deadlines and staying within budget.

Results:

The simulation might reveal that there is a 70% chance of completing the project within 12 months and a 60% chance of staying within the budget of $1 million. This insight allows the project manager and business owner to make informed decisions about resource allocation and contingency planning.

4.2.2 DECISION TREE ANALYSIS

Decision Tree Analysis is a graphical representation of decisions and their possible consequences, including risks, costs, and benefits. It helps project managers and business owners evaluate various options and choose the best course of action.

Example

Situation: Decision tree for a business owner considering expanding into a new market. The tree presented in this example includes options to expand now, wait for a year, or not expand at all, with associated risks and potential outcomes.

Step-by-Step Breakdown:

1. **Define the Decision Points:**
    - **Decision Point 1:** Expand now, wait for a year, or not expand.
2. **Identify Possible Outcomes:**
    - **Expand Now:**
        - **High Success:** High profit
        - **Moderate Success:** Moderate profit
        - **Failure:** Loss
    - **Wait for a Year:**
        - **High Success:** High profit

- **Moderate Success:** Moderate profit
- **Failure:** Loss
    - **Do Not Expand:**
        - **Status Quo:** No change in profit or loss
3. **Assign Probabilities and Payoffs:**
    - **Expand Now:**
        - **High Success:** Probability = 0.4, Payoff = $500,000
        - **Moderate Success:** Probability = 0.3, Payoff = $200,000
        - **Failure:** Probability = 0.3, Payoff = -$100,000
    - **Wait for a Year:**
        - **High Success:** Probability = 0.5, Payoff = $550,000
        - **Moderate Success:** Probability = 0.3, Payoff = $220,000
        - **Failure:** Probability = 0.2, Payoff = -$80,000
    - **Do Not Expand:**
        - **Status Quo:** Probability = 1.0, Payoff = $0
4. **Evaluate the Tree:**
    - **Expand Now:**
        - Expected Value = (0.4 * $500,000) + (0.3 * $200,000) + (0.3 * -$100,000)
        - Expected Value = $200,000 + $60,000 - $30,000 = $230,000
    - **Wait for a Year:**
        - Expected Value = (0.5 * $550,000) + (0.3 * $220,000) + (0.2 * -$80,000)
        - Expected Value = $275,000 + $66,000 - $16,000 = $325,000
    - **Do Not Expand:**
        - Expected Value = $0

Based on the expected values, waiting for a year has the highest expected value ($325,000).

Graphical view: The Decision Tree Diagram

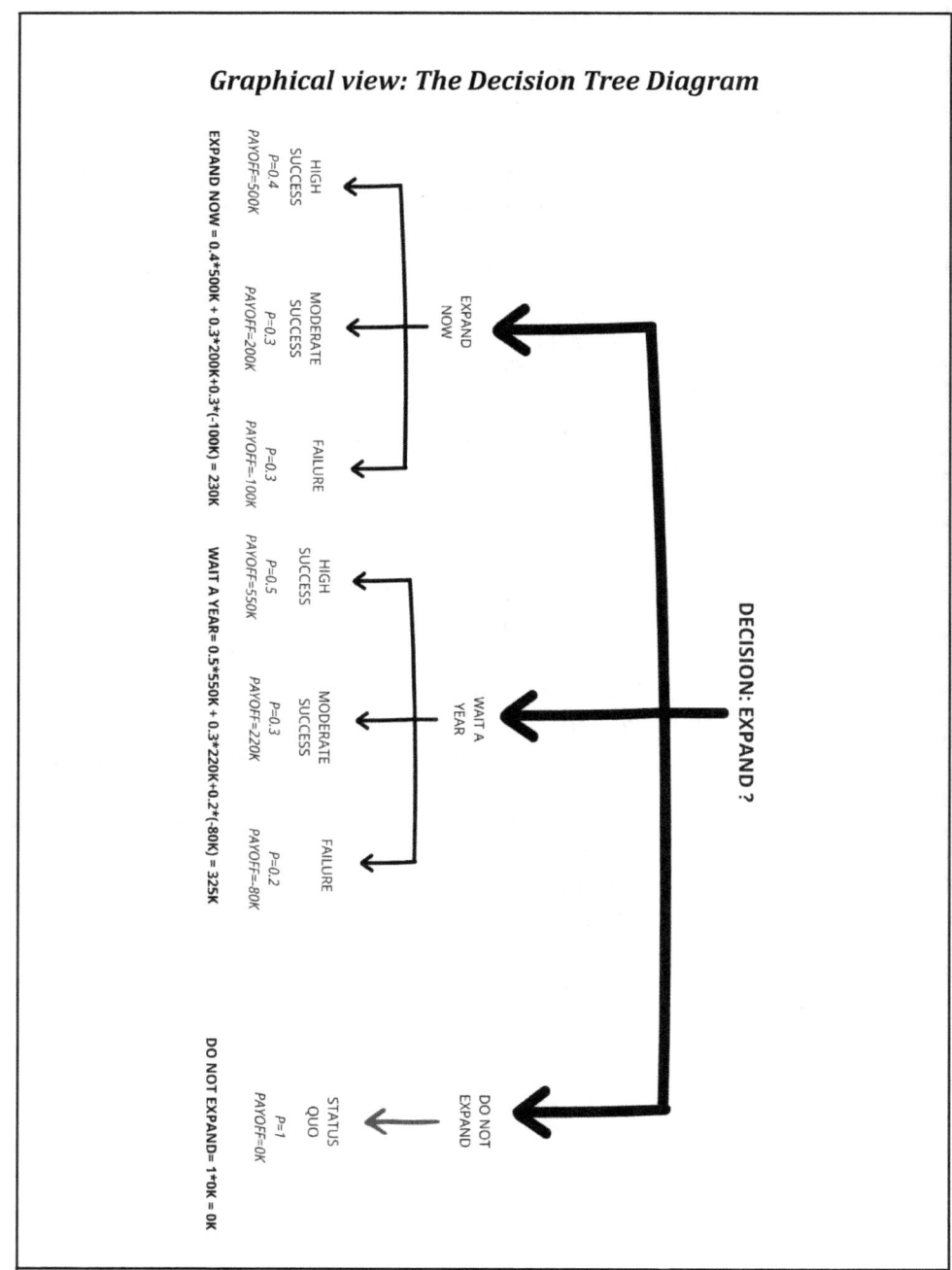

Explanation:

- ***Expand Now:*** Has a 40% chance of high success ($500,000), a 30% chance of moderate success ($200,000), and a 30% chance of failure (-$100,000). The expected value is $230,000.
- ***Wait for a Year:*** Has a 50% chance of high success ($550,000), a 30% chance of moderate success ($220,000), and a 20% chance of failure (-$80,000). The expected value is $325,000.
- ***Do Not Expand:*** No change, so the expected value is $0.

The best decision, based on this analysis, is to wait for a year before expanding into the new market.

4.2.3 SENSITIVITY ANALYSIS

Sensitivity Analysis assesses how changes in key variables impact project outcomes. It helps project managers and business owners understand which variables have the most significant effect on project performance and focus their risk management efforts accordingly.

Steps:

1. **Identify Key Variables:** Determine the critical variables that influence the project (e.g., material costs, labor rates, construction time).
2. **Analyze Impact:** Assess how changes in these variables impact the project outcome, typically using a model or simulation.
3. **Rank Variables:** Rank the variables based on their impact to identify the most sensitive factors.

Example

Scenario: A project manager is overseeing the construction of a new facility. They use sensitivity analysis to determine how variations in material costs, labor rates, and construction time affect the overall project cost.

Steps:

1. **Identify Key Variables:**
    - **Material Costs**
    - **Labor Rates**
    - **Construction Time**
2. **Analyze Impact:**
    - Develop a project cost model that includes the identified variables.
    - Use the model to simulate how changes in each variable impact the overall project cost.
    - For example, increase and decrease each variable by 10%, 20%, and 30% to see the effect on total costs.
3. **Rank Variables:**
    - Rank the variables based on the magnitude of their impact on the overall project cost.

Results:

- **Material Costs:**
    - 10% increase in material costs results in a $50,000 increase in project cost.
    - 20% increase results in a $100,000 increase.
    - 30% increase results in a $150,000 increase.
- **Labor Rates:**
    - 10% increase in labor rates results in a $30,000 increase in project cost.
    - 20% increase results in a $60,000 increase.
    - 30% increase results in a $90,000 increase.
- **Construction Time:**
    - 10% increase in construction time results in a $20,000 increase in project cost.
    - 20% increase results in a $40,000 increase.

- 30% increase results in a $60,000 increase.

Interpretation:

- **Ranking of Variables by Impact:**
    1. **Material Costs**
    2. **Labor Rates**
    3. **Construction Time**

The analysis reveals that material costs have the highest impact on the overall project cost, followed by labor rates and then construction time.

Conclusion:

By conducting sensitivity analysis, the project manager discovers that fluctuations in material costs significantly affect the total project cost. This insight allows them to prioritize monitoring and controlling material costs more closely to keep the project within budget. They might negotiate long-term contracts with suppliers to lock in prices, source alternative materials, or maintain a buffer stock to mitigate the risk of cost fluctuations.

Sensitivity Analysis Table:

Variable	+10% Impact	+20% Impact	+30% Impact
Material Costs	+$50,000	+$100,000	+$150,000
Labor Rates	+$30,000	+$60,000	+$90,000
Construction Time	+$20,000	+$40,000	+$60,000

This example illustrates how sensitivity analysis helps project managers understand the relative impact of different variables on project outcomes and focus their risk management efforts on the most critical factors.

Benefits of Quantitative Risk Assessment:

- **Accuracy:** Provides a more precise and objective evaluation of risks, aiding in better decision-making.
- **Forecasting:** Helps in predicting potential outcomes and preparing for various scenarios.
- **Resource Allocation:** Enables efficient allocation of resources based on quantified risks and their potential impacts.

All in all…

By leveraging quantitative risk assessment techniques such as Monte Carlo Simulation, Decision Tree Analysis, and Sensitivity Analysis, project managers and business owners can gain deeper insights into risks, make informed decisions, and enhance the likelihood of project success and business growth.

5 Risk Prioritization

Risk prioritization is the process of determining which risks require immediate attention and resources based on their potential impact on a project or business. By prioritizing risks, project managers and business owners can allocate resources more effectively, ensure critical risks are mitigated, and align risk management activities with strategic objectives.

Role of Project Managers and Business Owners:

- **Project Managers:** Lead the risk prioritization process within projects, ensuring that the most critical risks are addressed first to keep the project on track.
- **Business Owners:** Oversee risk prioritization at the organizational level, ensuring alignment with broader business goals and risk appetite.

5.1 Risk Ranking Methods

Risk ranking methods are techniques used to evaluate and prioritize risks based on their likelihood and impact. Common methods include:

1. Risk Matrix:

- A risk matrix is a visual tool that plots risks on a grid based on their likelihood and impact. Risks in the high-likelihood/high-impact quadrant are given the highest priority.

Example

> **Scenario:** *In a software development project, we have identified several risks and evaluated their likelihood and impact. These risks are then plotted*

on a risk matrix to prioritize them based on their severity.

Risk Categories:

- **High Likelihood, High Impact:** Requires immediate attention
- **High Likelihood, Medium Impact:** Needs proactive management
- **High Likelihood, Low Impact:** Monitor and manage
- **Medium Likelihood, High Impact:** Needs proactive management
- **Medium Likelihood, Medium Impact:** Monitor and manage
- **Medium Likelihood, Low Impact:** Monitor
- **Low Likelihood, High Impact:** Contingency planning
- **Low Likelihood, Medium Impact:** Monitor
- **Low Likelihood, Low Impact:** Acceptable risk, minimal monitoring

Identified Risks:

1. **Delays in key module delivery:** High Likelihood, High Impact
2. **Budget overruns:** Medium Likelihood, High Impact
3. **Minor software bugs:** High Likelihood, Low Impact
4. **Loss of key personnel:** Medium Likelihood, Medium Impact
5. **Server downtime:** Low Likelihood, High Impact
6. **Scope creep:** High Likelihood, Medium Impact
7. **Client requirement changes:** Medium Likelihood, Medium Impact
8. **Third-party integration issues:** Medium Likelihood, Low Impact
9. **Team productivity variance:** Low Likelihood, Medium Impact

Risk Matrix:

	Low Impact	**Medium Impact**	**High Impact**
High Likelihood	Minor software bugs	Scope creep	Delays in key module delivery
Medium Likelihood	Third-party integration issues	Loss of key personnel, Client requirement changes	Budget overruns
Low Likelihood	Acceptable risk	Team productivity variance	Server downtime

Interpretation:

- ***Delays in key module delivery (High Likelihood, High Impact):*** *This risk is in the highest priority quadrant. Immediate actions are required to mitigate this risk, such as closely monitoring progress and having contingency plans.*
- ***Budget overruns (Medium Likelihood, High Impact):*** *This risk needs proactive management. Regular budget reviews and cost control measures should be in place.*
- ***Minor software bugs (High Likelihood, Low Impact):*** *These are expected but low impact. Regular testing and bug fixing processes should handle this risk.*
- ***Loss of key personnel (Medium Likelihood, Medium Impact):*** *This needs monitoring and proactive measures such as cross-training and retention strategies.*
- ***Server downtime (Low Likelihood, High Impact):*** *Requires contingency planning like having a backup server and a disaster recovery plan.*
- ***Scope creep (High Likelihood, Medium Impact):*** *Proactive management is needed. Regular scope reviews and client communications are essential.*
- ***Client requirement changes (Medium Likelihood, Medium Impact):*** *Monitor and manage through change control processes and clear communication with the client.*
- ***Third-party integration issues (Medium Likelihood, Low Impact):*** *Monitor these issues and have regular checks with third-party vendors.*
- ***Team productivity variance (Low Likelihood, Medium Impact):*** *Monitor productivity and have plans in place to address any significant changes.*

This risk matrix helps in visually prioritizing and managing risks in the software development project by plotting them based on their likelihood and impact.

2. Scoring Systems:

- Risks are assigned scores based on predefined criteria for likelihood and impact. The scores are then summed or averaged to determine the overall risk level.

Example

Scenario: *A business is planning an expansion and has identified several risks. Each risk is scored based on predefined criteria for likelihood and impact. The scores are then summed to determine the overall risk level.*

Predefined Criteria for Scoring:

- **Likelihood:**
    - *1: Very Low*
    - *2: Low*
    - *3: Medium*
    - *4: High*
    - *5: Very High*
- **Impact:**
    - *1: Very Low*
    - *2: Low*
    - *3: Medium*
    - *4: High*
    - *5: Very High*

Identified Risks and Their Scores:

1. **Market demand fluctuation:**
    - *Likelihood: 3 (Medium)*
    - *Impact: 4 (High)*
    - *Overall Risk Score: 3 + 4 = 7*
2. **Regulatory changes:**
    - *Likelihood: 2 (Low)*
    - *Impact: 5 (Very High)*
    - *Overall Risk Score: 2 + 5 = 7*
3. **Operational scaling issues:**

- Likelihood: 4 (High)
- Impact: 3 (Medium)
- Overall Risk Score: 4 + 3 = 7
4. **Financial constraints:**
    - Likelihood: 3 (Medium)
    - Impact: 5 (Very High)
    - Overall Risk Score: 3 + 5 = 8
5. **Competition response:**
    - Likelihood: 4 (High)
    - Impact: 4 (High)
    - Overall Risk Score: 4 + 4 = 8
6. **Talent acquisition challenges:**
    - Likelihood: 2 (Low)
    - Impact: 3 (Medium)
    - Overall Risk Score: 2 + 3 = 5

Risk Scoring Table:

Risk	Likelihood Score	Impact Score	Overall Risk Score
Market demand fluctuation	3 (Medium)	4 (High)	7
Regulatory changes	2 (Low)	5 (Very High)	7
Operational scaling issues	4 (High)	3 (Medium)	7
Financial constraints	3 (Medium)	5 (Very High)	8
Competition response	4 (High)	4 (High)	8
Talent acquisition challenges	2 (Low)	3 (Medium)	5

Interpretation:

- **High-Priority Risks (Score: 8):**
    - **Financial constraints:** *Given a medium likelihood and very high impact, this risk should be addressed immediately with strong financial planning and securing adequate funding.*
    - **Competition response:** *With high likelihood and high impact, proactive competitive analysis and strategic planning are necessary to mitigate this risk.*
- **Medium-Priority Risks (Score: 7):**
    - **Market demand fluctuation:** *Medium likelihood and high impact require continuous market research and flexible business strategies to adapt to changing demand.*
    - **Regulatory changes:** *Low likelihood but very high impact necessitates staying informed about regulatory environments and having contingency plans.*
    - **Operational scaling issues:** *High likelihood and medium impact highlight the need for scalable processes and robust operational plans.*
- **Low-Priority Risk (Score: 5):**
    - **Talent acquisition challenges:** *Low likelihood and medium impact suggest that while this risk should be monitored, it may not need immediate action. Having a good recruitment and retention strategy will be beneficial.*

This scoring system provides a clear method for evaluating and prioritizing risks based on their likelihood and impact, helping project managers and business owners make informed decisions on which risks to address first.

3. Pareto Analysis (80/20 Rule):

- Focuses on identifying the 20% of risks that cause 80% of the problems. This method helps prioritize the most significant risks.

Example

Scenario: In a manufacturing project, the goal is to identify and prioritize the most significant risks (the 20% of risks that cause 80% of the problems) to prevent major production delays. By focusing on these key risks, the project manager can efficiently allocate resources to mitigate the most impactful issues.

Identified Risks and Their Impact:

1. **Equipment failure:** 40% of problems
2. **Supply chain disruptions:** 20% of problems
3. **Labor shortages:** 15% of problems
4. **Quality control issues:** 10% of problems
5. **Regulatory compliance:** 5% of problems
6. **Power outages:** 5% of problems
7. **Environmental factors:** 3% of problems
8. **Logistics delays:** 2% of problems

Pareto Analysis Table:

Risk	Impact (%)	Cumulative Impact (%)
Equipment failure	40%	40%
Supply chain disruptions	20%	60%
Labor shortages	15%	75%
Quality control issues	10%	85%
Regulatory compliance	5%	90%
Power outages	5%	95%
Environmental factors	3%	98%
Logistics delays	2%	100%

Interpretation and Action:

Top 20% of Risks (causing 80% of the problems):

1. **Equipment failure (40%):**
   - **Action:** Implement a robust maintenance schedule, invest in high-quality equipment, and have a rapid response team for repairs. This can prevent the majority of production delays due to equipment issues.
2. **Supply chain disruptions (20%):**
   - **Action:** Diversify suppliers, establish backup suppliers, and maintain buffer stock of critical materials. This reduces the impact of supply chain interruptions on production.
3. **Labor shortages (15%):**
   - **Action:** Improve hiring practices, provide competitive wages, and enhance working conditions to attract and retain skilled workers. Cross-training employees can also help cover labor shortages.
4. **Quality control issues (10%):**
   - **Action:** Implement stringent quality control processes, regular inspections, and employee training to maintain high production standards and reduce defects.

Remaining Risks (causing 20% of the problems):

5. **Regulatory compliance (5%):**
   - **Action:** Stay updated with regulations, conduct regular compliance audits, and provide training to ensure adherence to legal standards.
6. **Power outages (5%):**
   - **Action:** Invest in backup generators and uninterruptible power supplies (UPS) to keep operations running during power interruptions.
7. **Environmental factors (3%):**
   - **Action:** Assess environmental risks, implement protective measures, and have contingency plans for natural disasters or adverse weather conditions.
8. **Logistics delays (2%):**
   - **Action:** Optimize logistics processes, establish reliable transport partners, and plan for potential delays to minimize

> *their impact.*
>
> *By applying Pareto Analysis, the project manager can prioritize the most significant risks (equipment failure, supply chain disruptions, and labor shortages) and allocate resources effectively to mitigate these issues, thereby preventing the majority of production delays in the manufacturing project.*

4. Risk Urgency Assessment:

- Considers not only the likelihood and impact but also the timeframe within which the risk might occur. Urgent risks are prioritized higher.

Example

> **Scenario:** In a business expansion project, the goal is to assess risks based on their likelihood, impact, and the urgency or timeframe within which they might occur. By prioritizing urgent risks, the project manager can address immediate threats effectively.
>
> **Identified Risks and Their Scores:**
>
> 1. **Imminent regulatory change:**
>   - Likelihood: 4 (High)
>   - Impact: 5 (Very High)
>   - Urgency: 5 (Immediate)
>   - Overall Risk Score: (4 + 5) * 5 = 45
> 2. **Market demand fluctuation (short-term):**
>   - Likelihood: 3 (Medium)
>   - Impact: 4 (High)
>   - Urgency: 4 (Near-term)
>   - Overall Risk Score: (3 + 4) * 4 = 28
> 3. **Operational scaling issues:**
>   - Likelihood: 4 (High)
>   - Impact: 3 (Medium)

- Urgency: 3 (Medium-term)
- Overall Risk Score: (4 + 3) * 3 = 21
4. **Financial constraints:**
   - Likelihood: 3 (Medium)
   - Impact: 5 (Very High)
   - Urgency: 4 (Near-term)
   - Overall Risk Score: (3 + 5) * 4 = 32
5. **Competition response (long-term):**
   - Likelihood: 4 (High)
   - Impact: 4 (High)
   - Urgency: 2 (Long-term)
   - Overall Risk Score: (4 + 4) * 2 = 16
6. **Talent acquisition challenges:**
   - Likelihood: 2 (Low)
   - Impact: 3 (Medium)
   - Urgency: 3 (Medium-term)
   - Overall Risk Score: (2 + 3) * 3 = 15

Risk Urgency Assessment Table:

Risk	Likelihood Score	Impact Score	Urgency Score	Overall Risk Score
Imminent regulatory change	4 (High)	5 (Very High)	5 (Immediate)	45
Financial constraints	3 (Medium)	5 (Very High)	4 (Near-term)	32
Market demand fluctuation	3 (Medium)	4 (High)	4 (Near-term)	28
Operational scaling issues	4 (High)	3 (Medium)	3 (Medium-term)	21
Competition response	4 (High)	4 (High)	2 (Long-term)	16

| Talent acquisition challenges | 2 (Low) | 3 (Medium) | 3 (Medium-term) | 15 |

Interpretation:

- **Highest-Priority Risks:**
    - **Imminent regulatory change (Overall Score: 45):**
        - ***Action:*** *Immediate attention is required. Stay updated with regulatory changes, engage with legal experts, and ensure compliance plans are in place.*
    - **Financial constraints (Overall Score: 32):**
        - ***Action:*** *Near-term attention needed. Conduct financial analysis, secure funding, and implement cost control measures.*
    - **Market demand fluctuation (Overall Score: 28):**
        - ***Action:*** *Near-term attention required. Conduct market research, adapt marketing strategies, and maintain flexibility in operations.*
- **Medium-Priority Risks:**
    - **Operational scaling issues (Overall Score: 21):**
        - ***Action:*** *Medium-term attention needed. Develop scalable processes and ensure operational efficiency.*
    - **Competition response (Overall Score: 16):**
        - ***Action:*** *Long-term strategy required. Monitor competitors, innovate, and improve competitive positioning.*
- **Lower-Priority Risk:**
    - **Talent acquisition challenges (Overall Score: 15):**
        - ***Action:*** *Medium-term attention needed. Enhance recruitment strategies and create employee retention programs.*

By using a risk urgency assessment, the project manager can prioritize risks not just by their likelihood and impact but also by the urgency with which they must be addressed. This approach ensures that imminent and high-impact risks, such as regulatory changes and financial constraints, are given immediate attention, while long-term and lower-impact risks are

> *monitored and managed accordingly.*

5.2 RISK APPETITE AND TOLERANCE

Understanding and defining risk appetite and tolerance is crucial for effective risk prioritization. These concepts guide decision-making by setting the boundaries within which the organization is willing to operate.

1. Risk Appetite:

- Risk appetite is the amount and type of risk an organization is willing to pursue or retain to achieve its objectives. It reflects the organization's strategic goals and overall risk philosophy.

Example

Scenario: *Different organizations have varying levels of risk appetite based on their strategic goals, industry, and overall risk philosophy. Understanding and defining risk appetite helps these organizations align their risk-taking behaviors with their objectives.*

Examples of Organizations with Different Risk Appetites:

1. **Tech Startup:**
    - **Risk Appetite Level:** High
    - **Strategic Goals:** *Innovate rapidly, capture market share, disrupt existing markets.*
    - **Risk Philosophy:** *Willing to take significant risks, including financial, operational, and strategic risks, to achieve rapid growth and innovation.*
    - **Example Scenario:**
        - **Decision:** *Launch a new, untested product feature with the potential for high user adoption but also*

high failure risk.
- **Action:** Invest heavily in R&D, allocate resources to marketing, and prepare for rapid scaling or pivoting based on user feedback.
- **Outcome:** The startup accepts the risk of potential product failure in exchange for the opportunity to capture significant market share and establish itself as a leader in the industry.

2. **Healthcare Organization:**
   - **Risk Appetite Level:** Low
   - **Strategic Goals:** Ensure patient safety, comply with regulatory requirements, maintain high standards of care.
   - **Risk Philosophy:** Risk-averse, with a strong focus on minimizing any risks that could affect patient health, regulatory compliance, or the organization's reputation.
   - **Example Scenario:**
     - **Decision:** Implement a new electronic health records (EHR) system with proven reliability and compliance with healthcare regulations.
     - **Action:** Conduct thorough vendor evaluations, ensure extensive training for staff, and plan for a phased rollout to minimize disruptions.
     - **Outcome:** The healthcare organization chooses a conservative approach to ensure patient safety and compliance, accepting only minimal and well-managed risks.

Risk Appetite Table:

Organization Type	Risk Appetite Level	Strategic Goals	Risk Philosophy	Example Scenario
Tech Startup	High	Innovate rapidly, capture market share	Willing to take significant risks	Launch a new, untested product feature with high potential user adoption

				and high failure risk; invest heavily in R&D and marketing.
Healthcare Organization	Low	Ensure patient safety, comply with regulations	Risk-averse, focus on minimizing risks	Implement a new EHR system with proven reliability and compliance; conduct thorough evaluations and training; phased rollout to minimize disruptions.

Interpretation and Action:

- **High Risk Appetite:**
    - **Tech Startup:**
        - **Action:** *The startup should embrace innovative projects, be prepared for rapid changes, and allocate resources towards high-risk, high-reward initiatives. Regularly review and adjust the risk management strategy to align with fast-paced industry changes.*
- **Low Risk Appetite:**
    - **Healthcare Organization:**
        - **Action:** *The organization should prioritize patient safety and regulatory compliance, ensure thorough risk assessments, and implement risk mitigation strategies. Focus on reliable, proven technologies and methods to maintain high standards of care and compliance.*

Understanding and defining risk appetite is crucial for aligning an organization's risk-taking behavior with its strategic goals and overall risk philosophy. A tech startup with a high risk appetite can pursue aggressive growth and innovation strategies, accepting higher levels of risk. In contrast, a healthcare organization with a low risk appetite prioritizes patient safety and regulatory compliance, taking a conservative approach to risk management. By clearly defining their risk appetite, organizations can make informed decisions that support their objectives while managing risk effectively.

2. Risk Tolerance:

- Risk tolerance defines the acceptable level of variation around objectives that the organization is willing to withstand. It is more specific and operational than risk appetite.

Example

Scenario: Risk tolerance defines the specific level of variation from objectives that an organization is willing to accept. This concept is more precise and operational than risk appetite, guiding day-to-day decision-making.

Examples of Risk Tolerance in Different Contexts:

1. **Construction Project:**
    - **Risk Tolerance Level:** Low
    - **Objective:** Maintain project budget
    - **Risk Tolerance:** 5% budget overrun
    - **Example Scenario:**
        - **Decision:** A project manager sets a tolerance level where any cost overrun above 5% requires immediate mitigation.
        - **Action:** Closely monitor expenses, implement cost-control measures, and prepare contingency

plans for unexpected costs.
- **Outcome:** If the project faces a potential cost overrun of 6%, immediate actions are taken to mitigate this risk, such as negotiating with suppliers or reallocating resources.

2. **Tech Development Project:**
   - **Risk Tolerance Level:** Medium
   - **Objective:** Achieve project milestones on time
   - **Risk Tolerance:** 10% delay in milestone delivery
   - **Example Scenario:**
     - **Decision:** A software development project manager sets a tolerance level where any milestone delayed by more than 10% of the planned time frame requires intervention.
     - **Action:** Regularly review project timelines, allocate additional resources if delays are anticipated, and maintain flexibility in the project schedule.
     - **Outcome:** If a milestone is expected to be delayed by 12%, the project manager intervenes to address the delay, possibly by adding more team members or adjusting priorities.

3. **Marketing Campaign:**
   - **Risk Tolerance Level:** High
   - **Objective:** Achieve a specific ROI
   - **Risk Tolerance:** 20% variation in ROI
   - **Example Scenario:**
     - **Decision:** A marketing manager sets a tolerance level where any variation in the return on investment (ROI) beyond 20% of the target requires review and potential strategy adjustment.
     - **Action:** Monitor campaign performance metrics, adjust strategies based on real-time data, and experiment with different marketing tactics.
     - **Outcome:** If the campaign ROI deviates by 25%, the marketing manager reviews the campaign strategy and makes necessary adjustments to get back on track.

Risk Tolerance Table:

Project Type	Risk Tolerance Level	Objective	Risk Tolerance	Example Scenario
Construction Project	Low	Maintain project budget	5% budget overrun	Any cost overrun above 5% requires immediate mitigation; closely monitor expenses and implement cost-control measures.
Tech Development Project	Medium	Achieve project milestones on time	10% delay in milestones	Any milestone delayed by more than 10% requires intervention; review timelines, allocate resources, maintain schedule flexibility.
Marketing Campaign	High	Achieve specific ROI	20% variation in ROI	Any variation in ROI beyond 20% requires review; monitor performance metrics and adjust strategies as needed.

Interpretation and Action:

- ***Low Risk Tolerance:***
  - ***Construction Project:***
    - ***Action:*** *Implement stringent cost control measures, monitor expenses closely, and prepare contingency plans for unexpected costs. Immediate mitigation is required for any cost overrun beyond 5%.*
- ***Medium Risk Tolerance:***
  - ***Tech Development Project:***
    - ***Action:*** *Regularly review project timelines, be flexible with resource allocation, and intervene promptly if delays exceed 10%. Adjust priorities and add resources if necessary to stay on track.*
- ***High Risk Tolerance:***
  - ***Marketing Campaign:***
    - ***Action:*** *Monitor performance metrics continuously, be prepared to adjust strategies based on real-time data, and experiment with different tactics. Review and adjust the campaign strategy if ROI varies by more than 20%.*

Defining risk tolerance provides a clear and specific guideline for managing risk within acceptable limits. For a construction project, a low risk tolerance for budget overruns ensures strict cost control. In a tech development project, a medium risk tolerance allows for some flexibility in milestone delivery. For a marketing campaign, a high risk tolerance for ROI variations encourages adaptive strategies and experimentation. By setting clear risk tolerance levels, organizations can effectively manage risks while pursuing their objectives.

5.3 Prioritizing Risks in the Context of Business Objectives

Prioritizing risks involves aligning risk management activities with the business's strategic objectives. This ensures that resources are focused on risks that could significantly impact the achievement of key goals.

1. Align with Strategic Goals:

- Identify risks that directly affect the organization's ability to achieve its strategic goals and prioritize them accordingly.

Example

> *For a business aiming to expand internationally, geopolitical risks, and compliance with international regulations would be top priorities.*

2. Consider Stakeholder Expectations:

- Assess risks in light of stakeholder expectations and concerns. Prioritize risks that could impact customer satisfaction, investor confidence, or regulatory compliance.

Example

> *In a customer-centric company, risks affecting product quality and delivery times would be prioritized to maintain customer trust.*

3. Evaluate Resource Availability:

- Consider the availability of resources (financial, human, technological) when prioritizing risks. Focus on risks that can be effectively mitigated with available resources.

Example

> A small business with limited financial resources might prioritize risks related to cash flow and liquidity over long-term strategic risks.

4. Dynamic Reassessment:

- Regularly reassess and reprioritize risks as the project or business environment evolves. Ensure that the risk register reflects the current risk landscape and business priorities.

Example

> A project manager might reprioritize risks during a project review meeting, shifting focus to newly emerged risks such as sudden supplier issues or changes in market demand.

All in all…

By systematically prioritizing risks, project managers and business owners can ensure that the most significant risks are managed proactively, minimizing potential disruptions and enhancing the likelihood of achieving project and business objectives.

6 RISK RESPONSE PLANNING

Risk response planning involves developing strategies to address identified risks in a manner that aligns with project objectives and business goals. Effective risk response planning helps project managers and business owners minimize the impact of risks and seize opportunities that may arise.

Role of Project Managers and Business Owners:

- **Project Managers:** Lead the development and implementation of risk response strategies within projects, ensuring that risks are managed proactively and that the project stays on track.
- **Business Owners:** Provide strategic direction for risk response planning at the organizational level, ensuring that responses align with the overall business strategy and risk appetite.

OK so.. here we go again, this must be relevant... right?

Yes! Given the importance of this topic, we will provide further examples in addition to those already introduced in *Chapter 1.4 Key Terms and Definitions section 10. Risk Response Planning*.

6.1 NEGATIVE RISKS RESPONSES
6.1.1 RISK AVOIDANCE

Risk avoidance involves changing plans or processes to eliminate a risk or protect project objectives from its impact. This strategy is used when the risk has a high likelihood and a high impact, making it too dangerous to accept or mitigate.

Steps:

1. Identify risks that can be avoided.
2. Analyze the feasibility and implications of avoiding these risks.
3. Implement changes to eliminate the risks.

Example

> *Scenario: A project manager overseeing the construction of a new building identifies that the chosen site is prone to flooding. To avoid this risk, they decide to relocate the project to a different site with no flood risk.*
>
> *Results: By relocating the project, the risk of flooding is eliminated, ensuring that the construction project is not delayed or damaged by flood events.*

6.1.2 RISK MITIGATION

Risk mitigation involves taking actions to reduce the likelihood and/or impact of a risk to an acceptable level. This strategy is often used when the risk cannot be avoided but can be managed effectively through proactive measures.

Steps:

1. Identify potential mitigation actions.

2. Evaluate the effectiveness and cost of each action.

Implement the most effective mitigation actions.

Example

> *Scenario: A business owner launching a new product identifies a risk of supply chain disruptions. To mitigate this risk, they establish relationships with multiple suppliers and create a buffer stock of critical components.*
>
> *Results: The risk of supply chain disruptions is reduced by diversifying suppliers and maintaining buffer stock, ensuring that the product launch proceeds smoothly.*

6.1.3 RISK TRANSFER

Risk transfer involves shifting the impact of a risk to a third party. This is typically achieved through contracts, insurance, or other agreements. This strategy is useful when the risk can be managed more effectively by another party.

Steps:

1. Identify risks that can be transferred.
2. Determine the appropriate transfer mechanism (e.g., insurance, contracts).
3. Implement the transfer agreement.

Example

> *Scenario: A project manager for a software development project identifies the risk of data breaches. To transfer this risk, they purchase cybersecurity insurance and engage a third-party cybersecurity firm to manage data protection.*

> *Results: The financial impact of a potential data breach is transferred to the insurance company, and the responsibility for data protection is shared with a specialized cybersecurity firm, reducing the risk for the project.*

6.1.4 RISK ACCEPTANCE

Risk acceptance involves acknowledging the risk and deciding not to take any action unless the risk occurs. This strategy is used when the cost of mitigation exceeds the potential impact of the risk, or when the risk is within the organization's risk tolerance.

Steps:

1. Identify risks that can be accepted.
2. Evaluate the potential impact and likelihood.
3. Document the decision to accept the risk and monitor it.

Example

> *Scenario: A business owner is aware of a minor risk of a slight increase in material costs for a small project. Given the low likelihood and impact, they decide to accept this risk without taking specific actions.*
>
> *Results: By accepting the minor risk of increased material costs, the business owner avoids unnecessary mitigation expenses while keeping an eye on cost fluctuations.*

6.2 Positive Risks Responses

6.2.1 Risk Exploitation

In this case, we take actions to ensure that the opportunity is realized. This involves making proactive decisions to guarantee that the positive risk occurs.

Steps:

- Identify opportunities that can be exploited.
- Analyze the feasibility and potential benefits of exploiting these opportunities.
- Implement actions to ensure the opportunity is realized.

Example

> **Scenario:** *A software development company identifies an opportunity to be the first to market with a new, innovative product. To exploit this opportunity, the company allocates additional resources and prioritizes the project to ensure it meets the market deadline.*
>
> **Results:** *By expediting the project, the company captures a significant market share, leading to increased revenue and brand recognition.*

6.2.2 Risk Enhancement

Here we will try to increase the probability and/or positive impact of the opportunity. This involves taking actions to maximize the likelihood of the opportunity occurring or its beneficial impact.

Steps:

- Identify opportunities that can be enhanced.

- Assess the potential to increase the probability or impact of these opportunities.
- Implement actions to enhance the opportunity.

Example:

Scenario: *A project manager discovers that an emerging technology could significantly improve project efficiency. The project manager invests in additional training for the team to quickly adapt and integrate the new technology.*

Results: *The improved efficiency reduces project completion time and costs, resulting in higher profitability and client satisfaction.*

6.2.3 RISK SHARING

Allocate ownership of the opportunity to a third party who is better positioned to achieve the benefits. This involves collaborating with others to maximize the potential of the opportunity.

Steps:

- Identify opportunities that can be shared.
- Determine the appropriate third party to share the opportunity with.
- Develop agreements to share the benefits.

Example

> **Scenario:** A small business identifies a market expansion opportunity but lacks the resources to capitalize on it fully. The business partners with a larger company that has the necessary resources and market presence.
>
> **Results:** By sharing the opportunity, both companies benefit from increased market reach and revenue growth.

6.2.4 RISK ACCEPTANCE

In this case we will acknowledge the opportunity and take advantage of it if it occurs. This involves being open to the opportunity but not taking any proactive steps to ensure it happens.

Steps:

- Identify opportunities that can be accepted.
- Evaluate the potential benefits and likelihood.
- Monitor the situation and be prepared to act if the opportunity arises.

Example

> **Scenario:** A business owner is aware of a potential increase in demand for their products due to an upcoming trend. The business owner decides to maintain current operations and be ready to scale up production if the demand increases.
>
> **Results:** By accepting the opportunity, the business owner avoids unnecessary investments but remains prepared to capitalize on the trend if it materializes.

6.3 Contingency Planning

Contingency planning involves developing plans to execute if a risk event occurs. This ensures that the project or business can quickly and effectively respond to risks, minimizing disruption and maintaining progress towards objectives.

Steps:

1. Identify potential risk events that require contingency plans.
2. Develop detailed plans for each identified risk.
3. Communicate the contingency plans to relevant stakeholders and ensure readiness.

Example

> *Scenario: A project manager for an international construction project identifies the risk of political instability in the project country. They develop a contingency plan that includes alternative suppliers, evacuation plans for staff, and temporary relocation of project activities.*
>
> *Results: If political instability arises, the project manager can implement the contingency plan, ensuring the safety of staff and the continuity of project activities.*

Benefits of Risk Response Planning:

- **Proactive Management:** Allows project managers and business owners to address risks before they become issues.
- **Resource Optimization:** Ensures resources are allocated effectively to manage risks.

- **Enhanced Resilience:** Improves the organization's ability to withstand and recover from risk events.

All in all…

By effectively planning for and responding to risks, project managers and business owners can enhance the likelihood of achieving their objectives, maintaining project timelines, and safeguarding business interests.

7 Implementing Risk Management Strategies

Effective risk management requires not only planning but also robust implementation. Implementing risk management strategies involves assigning responsibilities, developing actionable plans, and integrating risk management into daily business operations.

Role of Project Managers and Business Owners:

- **Project Managers:** Ensure that risk management strategies are effectively implemented within projects, coordinating efforts and tracking progress.
- **Business Owners:** Oversee the integration of risk management into the broader business strategy, fostering a culture of proactive risk management across the organization.

7.1 Assigning Risk Owners

Assigning risk owners is crucial to ensure that each risk has a designated individual responsible for its management. Risk owners are accountable for monitoring, reporting, and mitigating their assigned risks.

Steps to Assign Risk Owners:

1. **Identify Risks:** Review the risk register to identify all significant risks.
2. **Select Risk Owners:** Assign each risk to a specific individual based on their expertise, authority, and ability to manage the risk effectively.
3. **Define Responsibilities:** Clearly outline the responsibilities of each risk owner, including monitoring, reporting, and implementing mitigation strategies.
4. **Communicate Assignments:** Inform all stakeholders of the risk owners and their responsibilities.

Example

> *In a software development project, the project manager assigns the risk of "server downtime" to the IT lead. The IT lead is responsible for monitoring server performance, reporting potential issues, and implementing measures to minimize downtime.*

7.2 Developing Risk Action Plans

Risk action plans detail the steps that will be taken to address identified risks. These plans include specific actions, timelines, resources required, and success criteria.

Steps to Develop Risk Action Plans:

1. **Identify Actions:** Determine the specific actions needed to address each risk, such as mitigation, transfer, acceptance, or avoidance strategies.
2. **Assign Responsibilities:** Assign each action to a responsible individual or team, typically the risk owner.
3. **Set Timelines:** Define clear timelines for implementing the actions.

4. **Allocate Resources:** Ensure that the necessary resources (financial, human, technological) are allocated to execute the action plans.
5. **Establish Success Criteria:** Define the criteria for measuring the success of the actions taken.

Example

> *A business owner in the retail industry develops an action plan to address the risk of supply chain disruptions. The plan includes actions such as diversifying suppliers, increasing inventory levels, and implementing a supply chain monitoring system. Each action is assigned to the supply chain manager, with specific deadlines and allocated resources.*

7.3 INTEGRATING RISK MANAGEMENT INTO BUSINESS PROCESSES

Integrating risk management into business processes ensures that risk management is a continuous and systematic part of organizational operations. This integration helps in early identification and effective management of risks.

Steps to Integrate Risk Management:

1. **Embed Risk Management in Strategic Planning:** Incorporate risk management considerations into the organization's strategic planning and decision-making processes.
2. **Align with Business Processes:** Align risk management activities with existing business processes, such as project management, financial planning, and operational workflows.
3. **Develop Policies and Procedures:** Establish policies and procedures that guide risk management activities across the organization.

4. **Foster a Risk-Aware Culture:** Promote a culture of risk awareness and proactive risk management through training, communication, and leadership support.
5. **Monitor and Review:** Continuously monitor risk management activities and review their effectiveness, making adjustments as necessary.

Example

> *A project manager in a construction company integrates risk management into the project planning process by conducting risk assessments during the initial planning phase. The project manager ensures that risk management activities are included in the project schedule, budget, and resource allocation. Regular risk reviews are conducted to monitor progress and make necessary adjustments.*

Benefits of Implementing Risk Management Strategies:

- **Enhanced Accountability:** Assigning risk owners ensures that risks are actively managed and monitored.
- **Effective Mitigation:** Developing risk action plans enables systematic and targeted risk mitigation efforts.
- **Seamless Integration:** Integrating risk management into business processes ensures that risk considerations are part of everyday operations, enhancing overall resilience.

All in all…

By effectively implementing risk management strategies, project managers and business owners can create a structured approach to managing risks, ensuring that risks are identified, assessed, and addressed in a timely and effective manner.

8 Monitoring and Reviewing Risks

Monitoring and reviewing risks is an essential part of the risk management process. It ensures that risks are continuously assessed, tracked, and managed effectively. Regular monitoring and reviews enable project managers and business owners to respond promptly to changes and maintain control over potential risks.

Role of Project Managers and Business Owners:

- **Project Managers:** Responsible for ongoing monitoring of project-specific risks and ensuring that risk responses are effective.
- **Business Owners:** Oversee the continuous assessment of strategic and operational risks at the organizational level, ensuring alignment with business objectives.

8.1 Continuous Risk Monitoring

Continuous risk monitoring involves the ongoing observation and tracking of identified risks and their associated response actions. This proactive approach helps in detecting changes in risk conditions and ensuring timely interventions.

Steps for Continuous Risk Monitoring:

1. **Establish Monitoring Mechanisms:** Set up systems and processes to regularly collect and analyze risk-related data.
2. **Track Risk Indicators:** Monitor key indicators that signal changes in risk likelihood or impact.
3. **Document Observations:** Maintain detailed records of risk observations and any changes in risk status.
4. **Report Findings:** Communicate monitoring results to relevant stakeholders, including risk owners and management.

Example

> *In an IT project, the project manager uses automated monitoring tools to track system performance and identify potential risks such as server overload or security breaches. Regular reports are generated and reviewed to ensure early detection and mitigation of risks.*

8.2 Key Risk Indicators (KRIs)

Key Risk Indicators (KRIs) are metrics used to measure and track the potential impact of identified risks. KRIs provide early warning signals, enabling organizations to take proactive measures before risks materialize.

Steps to Implement KRIs:

1. **Identify Relevant KRIs:** Determine the most critical indicators that reflect the status of key risks.
2. **Set Thresholds:** Establish acceptable threshold levels for each KRI to trigger alerts when exceeded.
3. **Monitor Regularly:** Continuously track KRIs and compare them against thresholds.
4. **Analyze Trends:** Analyze KRI data to identify patterns and trends that may indicate emerging risks.
5. **Respond to Alerts:** Take immediate action when KRIs exceed thresholds, including re-evaluating risk responses.

Example

> *A business owner in the manufacturing industry monitors KRIs such as machinery downtime, defect rates, and supplier delivery delays. When defect*

> rates exceed the set threshold, immediate quality control measures are implemented to address the issue.

8.3 Periodic Risk Reviews

Periodic risk reviews are scheduled assessments conducted to evaluate the effectiveness of risk management activities and update risk information. These reviews help ensure that risk management remains relevant and aligned with project or business changes.

Steps for Conducting Periodic Risk Reviews:

1. **Schedule Reviews:** Determine the frequency of risk reviews (e.g., monthly, quarterly) based on the complexity and duration of the project or business operations.
2. **Gather Data:** Collect up-to-date information on identified risks, KRIs, and risk response actions.
3. **Evaluate Effectiveness:** Assess the effectiveness of implemented risk responses and identify any gaps.
4. **Update Risk Register:** Revise the risk register to reflect current risk statuses, new risks, and changes in existing risks.
5. **Communicate Findings:** Share review outcomes with stakeholders and update them on any changes to risk management plans.

Example

> *A project manager in a construction project conducts quarterly risk reviews to assess the impact of seasonal weather changes on project timelines. Based*

> *on the review findings, the project schedule is adjusted, and additional resources are allocated to mitigate weather-related risks.*

8.4 Adjusting Risk Responses

Adjusting risk responses involves modifying existing strategies or developing new actions based on the outcomes of risk monitoring and reviews. This ensures that risk management remains dynamic and responsive to changing conditions.

Steps to Adjust Risk Responses:

1. **Identify Changes:** Determine if there are any changes in risk likelihood, impact, or new risks that have emerged.
2. **Evaluate Current Responses:** Assess whether current risk responses are still effective and appropriate.
3. **Develop Adjustments:** Plan necessary adjustments to existing risk responses or develop new strategies.
4. **Implement Changes:** Execute the adjusted risk responses and ensure they are integrated into project or business operations.
5. **Monitor Adjustments:** Continuously monitor the effectiveness of the adjusted responses to ensure they achieve the desired outcomes.

Example

> *A business owner in the retail sector identifies a sudden market shift due to economic downturns. The current risk response plan focused on inventory management is adjusted to include aggressive marketing campaigns and discount strategies to maintain sales and customer engagement.*

Benefits of Monitoring and Reviewing Risks:

- **Early Detection:** Continuous monitoring allows for early identification of potential risks, enabling proactive management.
- **Improved Decision-Making:** Regular reviews provide updated risk information, supporting informed decision-making.
- **Dynamic Response:** Adjusting risk responses ensures that risk management strategies remain effective and relevant in changing environments.
- **Enhanced Control:** Ongoing risk assessment and monitoring enhance the organization's ability to manage risks and achieve objectives.

All in all...

By implementing robust monitoring and review processes, project managers and business owners can ensure that risks are managed effectively, keeping projects and business operations on track and resilient against uncertainties.

9 COMMUNICATION AND REPORTING

Effective communication and reporting are vital components of risk management. They ensure that all stakeholders are informed about potential risks, their impacts, and the actions being taken to manage them. This transparency fosters trust and enables better decision-making.

Role of Project Managers and Business Owners:

- **Project Managers:** Responsible for conveying risk-related information to project stakeholders, ensuring they are aware of potential risks and mitigation strategies.

- **Business Owners:** Communicate risk management policies and updates to senior management, investors, and other key stakeholders, promoting a risk-aware culture across the organization.

9.1 Communicating Risk to Stakeholders

Communicating risk to stakeholders involves sharing relevant risk information in a clear, concise, and timely manner. This helps stakeholders understand the potential impacts and the measures in place to address them.

Steps for Effective Risk Communication:

1. **Identify Stakeholders:** Determine who needs to be informed about risk-related issues, including internal team members, clients, investors, and regulatory bodies.
2. **Tailor Communication:** Customize the level of detail and complexity of risk information based on the audience's needs and their level of expertise.
3. **Choose Appropriate Channels:** Select the most effective communication channels, such as meetings, reports, emails, or presentations.
4. **Be Transparent:** Provide honest and clear information about the nature of the risks, their potential impacts, and the actions being taken.
5. **Engage Stakeholders:** Encourage feedback and discussion to ensure stakeholders understand the risks and feel involved in the risk management process.

Example

> *A project manager working on a software development project holds regular meetings with the client to discuss identified risks, such as potential delays due to third-party dependencies. The project manager explains the risks, outlines the mitigation strategies, and provides updates on progress.*

9.2 Risk Reporting Tools and Techniques

Using appropriate tools and techniques for risk reporting ensures that risk information is organized, accessible, and actionable. These tools help in tracking, analyzing, and presenting risk data effectively.

Common Risk Reporting Tools and Techniques:

1. **Risk Register:** A comprehensive document that lists all identified risks, their assessments, and response plans. It is regularly updated and reviewed.
2. **Risk Heat Maps:** Visual representations that show the likelihood and impact of risks, helping to prioritize them based on their severity.
3. **Dashboards:** Interactive digital interfaces that provide real-time updates on key risk indicators and risk management activities.
4. **Risk Reports:** Detailed documents that provide insights into the status of risks, their potential impacts, and the effectiveness of mitigation strategies.
5. **Gantt Charts:** Visual timelines that illustrate project schedules, including tasks related to risk management.

Example

Scenario: Risk heat map for a software development project:

1. **Risk Identification:**
    - **High Likelihood, High Impact:** Delays in key module delivery.
    - **High Likelihood, Medium Impact:** High turnover rate among developers.
    - **Medium Likelihood, High Impact:** Significant security vulnerabilities discovered late.
    - **Low Likelihood, High Impact:** Major changes in regulatory requirements.
    - **Medium Likelihood, Medium Impact:** Budget overruns.
    - **Low Likelihood, Medium Impact:** Minor integration issues.
    - **High Likelihood, Low Impact:** Minor bugs in the codebase.
    - **Medium Likelihood, Low Impact:** Delays in receiving feedback from stakeholders.
    - **Low Likelihood, Low Impact:** Minor documentation errors.

Steps to Create the Risk Heat Map:

1. **Define the Risk Matrix:**
    - **Likelihood Levels:** High, Medium, Low.
    - **Impact Levels:** High, Medium, Low.
2. **Assign Risks to the Matrix:**
    - **High Likelihood, High Impact:** Delays in key module delivery.
    - **High Likelihood, Medium Impact:** High turnover rate among developers.
    - **Medium Likelihood, High Impact:** Significant security vulnerabilities discovered late.
    - **Low Likelihood, High Impact:** Major changes in regulatory requirements.
    - **Medium Likelihood, Medium Impact:** Budget overruns.
    - **Low Likelihood, Medium Impact:** Minor integration issues.

    - **High Likelihood, Low Impact:** Minor bugs in the codebase.
    - **Medium Likelihood, Low Impact:** Delays in receiving feedback from stakeholders.
    - **Low Likelihood, Low Impact:** Minor documentation errors.

Visual Representation. The Risk Heat Map:

Impact / Likelihood	High	Medium	Low
High	Delays in key module delivery	Significant security vulnerabilities discovered late	Major changes in regulatory requirements
Medium	High turnover rate among developers	Budget overruns	Minor integration issues
Low	Minor bugs in the codebase	Delays in receiving feedback from stakeholders	Minor documentation errors

In this matrix:

- *Risks in the top-right quadrant (High Likelihood, High Impact) require immediate attention.*
- *Risks in the middle are of medium concern and should be monitored closely.*
- *Risks in the bottom-left quadrant (Low Likelihood, Low Impact) are of lower priority but still should be tracked.*

You can create this heat map using various tools, such as Excel, project management software, or specialized risk management tools.

9.3 Building a Risk-Aware Culture

Building a risk-aware culture involves creating an environment where employees at all levels understand the importance of risk management and are actively engaged in identifying and managing risks.

Steps to Build a Risk-Aware Culture:

1. **Leadership Commitment:** Ensure that senior management demonstrates a strong commitment to risk management, setting the tone for the rest of the organization.
2. **Training and Education:** Provide regular training sessions to educate employees about risk management principles, tools, and their role in the process.
3. **Encourage Open Communication:** Foster an environment where employees feel comfortable discussing risks and reporting potential issues without fear of retribution.
4. **Integrate Risk Management:** Embed risk management practices into daily operations and decision-making processes across the organization.
5. **Recognize and Reward:** Acknowledge and reward proactive risk management behaviors to encourage ongoing engagement and commitment.

Example

A business owner in the healthcare industry implements a comprehensive risk management training program for all staff members. The training covers risk identification, assessment, and response techniques. Additionally, the owner encourages open discussions about risks during team meetings and recognizes employees who proactively manage risks.

Benefits of Effective Communication and Reporting:

- **Informed Decision-Making:** Stakeholders have the information they need to make well-informed decisions.
- **Transparency and Trust:** Clear and honest communication fosters trust among stakeholders.
- **Proactive Risk Management:** Regular reporting and open communication enable early identification and mitigation of risks.
- **Enhanced Engagement:** Building a risk-aware culture ensures that all employees are engaged in risk management, leading to a more resilient organization.

All in all…

By prioritizing effective communication and reporting, project managers and business owners can ensure that risks are managed transparently and collaboratively, enhancing the overall effectiveness of the risk management process.

10 Advanced Topics in Risk Management

Although this is an introductory book on risk management, we want to introduce you to some advanced approaches. You'll find that they are not much different from what we have covered so far, but it is important to be familiar with them.

10.1 Enterprise Risk Management (ERM)

Enterprise Risk Management (ERM) is a comprehensive approach to identifying, assessing, and managing risks across an entire organization. For project managers and business owners, ERM is essential for aligning risk management practices with strategic goals and ensuring that all types of risks are addressed effectively.

Key Components of ERM:

- **Risk Governance:** Establish a structured framework defining roles, responsibilities, and processes for managing risks across the organization. For example, a risk committee comprising senior executives might oversee risk management activities, while project managers identify and manage risks within their specific projects.
- **Risk Appetite and Tolerance:** Determine the level of risk the organization is willing to accept in pursuit of its objectives. For instance, a tech startup might have a high tolerance for innovation-related risks but a low tolerance for financial risks. Business owners and project managers should align their risk management strategies with these thresholds.
- **Risk Assessment:** Identify, analyze, and prioritize risks. Techniques such as SWOT analysis (Strengths, Weaknesses, Opportunities, Threats) and risk matrices are commonly used. For example, a project manager can use a risk matrix to assess potential delays in a construction project, while a business owner might conduct a SWOT analysis to evaluate market expansion risks.

- **Risk Response:** Develop strategies to mitigate, transfer, avoid, or accept risks. A project manager might create a contingency plan for potential equipment failures, while a business owner might transfer risk by purchasing insurance for natural disasters.
- **Risk Monitoring and Reporting:** Continuously monitor risks and the effectiveness of risk responses. For instance, project managers should track key risk indicators (KRIs) and report to stakeholders regularly. Business owners might use dashboards to monitor enterprise-wide risks and ensure transparency.

Example

Scenario: *A mid-sized manufacturing company, XYZ Manufacturing, seeks to implement Enterprise Risk Management (ERM) to better align its risk management practices with its strategic goals and ensure comprehensive management of risks across the organization. The company produces automotive parts and has recently decided to expand its product line and enter new markets.*

Key Components of ERM Implementation:

1. **Risk Governance:**
   - **Establishment:** *XYZ Manufacturing establishes a Risk Committee comprising senior executives, including the CEO, CFO, COO, and heads of key departments such as Production, Quality Assurance, and R&D. This committee is responsible for overseeing risk management activities across the organization.*
   - **Roles and Responsibilities:** *Project managers within each department are tasked with identifying and managing risks specific to their projects, while the Risk Committee ensures that these efforts are aligned with the organization's overall risk management strategy.*
2. **Risk Appetite and Tolerance:**
   - **Determination:** *The Risk Committee determines that XYZ Manufacturing has a moderate risk appetite, willing to accept innovation-related risks to stay competitive but*

maintaining a low tolerance for financial risks and regulatory compliance issues.
- **Alignment:** Business owners and project managers align their risk management strategies accordingly. For example, the R&D department is encouraged to pursue innovative projects, but all initiatives must be carefully evaluated for financial feasibility and regulatory compliance.

3. **Risk Assessment:**
   - **Techniques Used:** The Risk Committee employs SWOT analysis and risk matrices to identify, analyze, and prioritize risks.
   - **Application:**
     - **SWOT Analysis:** A SWOT analysis is conducted to evaluate the risks associated with expanding into the electric vehicle (EV) market. Strengths include the company's established brand and strong R&D capabilities; weaknesses involve limited experience in the EV market. Opportunities lie in the growing demand for EVs, while threats include intense competition and regulatory challenges.
     - **Risk Matrix:** A risk matrix is used to assess potential delays in the production of a new product line. Risks are plotted based on their likelihood and impact, with high-likelihood/high-impact risks prioritized for immediate attention.

4. **Risk Response:**
   - **Strategies Developed:** The company develops various risk response strategies, including mitigation, transfer, avoidance, and acceptance.
   - **Examples:**
     - **Mitigation:** To address the risk of equipment failures, the production department creates a maintenance schedule and procures backup machinery.
     - **Transfer:** To manage the risk of natural disasters, the company purchases comprehensive insurance coverage.
     - **Avoidance:** The company decides against entering a highly unstable foreign market, thereby avoiding

> potential political and economic risks.
> - **Acceptance:** Minor fluctuations in raw material prices are accepted as part of normal business operations, with no specific actions taken.
> 5. **Risk Monitoring and Reporting:**
>   - **Monitoring:** Key Risk Indicators (KRIs) are established for critical risks, such as production delays and regulatory compliance issues. These KRIs are monitored continuously by project managers and reported to the Risk Committee monthly.
>   - **Reporting:** The Risk Committee uses dashboards to monitor enterprise-wide risks and ensure transparency. Regular risk reports are provided to all stakeholders, highlighting current risk levels and the effectiveness of risk responses.
>
> *Implementing Enterprise Risk Management (ERM) at XYZ Manufacturing has led to a more structured and proactive approach to managing risks. The company benefits from improved decision-making, enhanced risk awareness, increased resilience, and better regulatory compliance. By aligning risk management practices with its strategic goals, XYZ Manufacturing is well-positioned to navigate challenges and capitalize on opportunities in the competitive manufacturing industry.*

Benefits of ERM:

- **Improved Decision-Making:** With a comprehensive understanding of risks, project managers and business owners can make better-informed decisions that align with the organization's risk appetite.
- **Enhanced Risk Awareness:** ERM promotes a culture of risk awareness, encouraging proactive identification and management of risks at all levels.
- **Increased Resilience:** By addressing a broad range of risks, organizations become more resilient to adverse events and can recover more quickly.

- **Regulatory Compliance:** ERM helps organizations comply with regulatory requirements, reducing the risk of legal penalties and fines.

10.2 Cybersecurity Risk Management

Cybersecurity risk management focuses on protecting information technology systems and data from cyber threats. Given the increasing sophistication of cyberattacks, managing cybersecurity risks is critical for both project managers and business owners.

Key Components of Cybersecurity Risk Management:

- **Risk Identification:** Identify potential cyber threats and vulnerabilities. For example, a project manager overseeing a software development project might identify risks such as unauthorized access or data breaches. A business owner might identify risks associated with storing customer data online.
- **Risk Assessment:** Evaluate the likelihood and potential impact of identified risks. This can include vulnerability assessments and penetration testing. For instance, a project manager might conduct a penetration test to identify weaknesses in a new application, while a business owner assesses the potential impact of a data breach on customer trust.
- **Risk Mitigation:** Implement measures to reduce the likelihood or impact of cyber threats. This can include technical controls like firewalls and encryption, administrative controls like policies and training, and physical controls like secure facilities. A project manager might ensure that all team members receive cybersecurity training, while a business owner might implement multi-factor authentication for accessing sensitive data.
- **Incident Response:** Develop and implement a plan to respond to cybersecurity incidents. This includes identifying the incident, containing the threat, eradicating the cause, and recovering from the

impact. For example, a project manager might have a response plan for a ransomware attack, while a business owner ensures a robust backup system is in place to recover lost data.
- **Continuous Monitoring:** Continuously monitor IT systems for signs of cyber threats. This includes using intrusion detection systems, security information and event management (SIEM) systems, and regular security audits. A project manager might use real-time monitoring tools to detect anomalies, while a business owner ensures regular audits to maintain security standards.

Best Practices in Cybersecurity Risk Management:

- **Adopt a Risk-Based Approach:** Focus on the most critical assets and threats, and allocate resources based on risk priorities. For example, a project manager might prioritize securing the most sensitive data, while a business owner focuses on protecting critical business systems.
- **Regularly Update Security Measures:** Cyber threats evolve rapidly, so it's essential to keep security measures up to date. Both project managers and business owners should ensure their teams are aware of the latest threats and mitigation techniques.
- **Promote a Security-Aware Culture:** Educate employees about cybersecurity best practices and encourage them to report suspicious activities. Regular training sessions and awareness programs can help in fostering a security-aware culture.
- **Collaborate with Stakeholders:** Work with IT, legal, and compliance teams to ensure a comprehensive approach to cybersecurity. For instance, project managers might collaborate with IT teams to implement security controls, while business owners ensure compliance with legal requirements.

10.3 Risk Management in Agile Projects

Agile project management emphasizes flexibility, collaboration, and iterative progress, presenting unique challenges and opportunities for risk management.

Key Components of Risk Management in Agile Projects:

- **Iterative Risk Assessment:** Regularly assess risks at the beginning of each iteration (sprint). This ensures that new risks are identified and addressed promptly. For example, a project manager might hold a risk assessment meeting at the start of each sprint to identify potential obstacles.
- **Collaborative Risk Management:** Involve the entire project team in risk identification and mitigation. Agile practices such as daily stand-ups and retrospectives provide opportunities for continuous risk discussion. For instance, team members can share concerns during daily stand-ups, allowing the project manager to address them immediately.
- **Adaptive Risk Responses:** Develop flexible risk responses that can be adjusted as the project evolves. Agile's iterative nature allows for rapid adjustments to risk management strategies. For example, if a critical feature is causing delays, the project manager can reprioritize tasks in the next sprint to mitigate the impact.
- **Transparency and Communication:** Maintain open communication about risks within the team and with stakeholders. Agile practices encourage frequent feedback and collaboration, which supports effective risk management. Regular updates and transparent reporting help in building trust and ensuring that everyone is aware of potential risks.

Benefits of Agile Risk Management:

- **Enhanced Flexibility:** Agile's iterative approach allows teams to adapt to changes and address risks more quickly. This flexibility helps in managing uncertainties and ensures project success.

- **Improved Team Engagement:** Collaborative risk management fosters a sense of ownership and accountability among team members. When everyone is involved in risk management, it leads to better engagement and more effective mitigation strategies.
- **Better Risk Visibility:** Regular risk assessments and open communication ensure that risks are promptly identified and addressed. This visibility helps in preventing issues from escalating and ensures timely interventions.
- **Continuous Improvement:** Agile practices such as retrospectives support continuous improvement in risk management processes. Teams can learn from past experiences and implement changes to improve risk management in future sprints.

10.4 RISK MANAGEMENT AND REGULATORY COMPLIANCE

Regulatory compliance involves adhering to laws, regulations, and standards that apply to an organization's operations. Effective risk management is essential for ensuring compliance and avoiding legal and financial penalties.

Key Components of Risk Management for Regulatory Compliance:

- **Identify Relevant Regulations:** Understand the laws and regulations that apply to the organization. This includes industry-specific regulations, data protection laws, and environmental standards. For instance, a business owner in the healthcare sector must comply with HIPAA regulations, while a project manager might need to adhere to industry standards like ISO.
- **Conduct Compliance Risk Assessments:** Evaluate the organization's exposure to compliance risks. This involves identifying potential areas of non-compliance and assessing their impact. For example, a business owner might assess risks related to GDPR

compliance, while a project manager evaluates risks associated with meeting contractual obligations.
- **Implement Compliance Controls:** Develop and implement controls to mitigate compliance risks. This includes policies, procedures, training programs, and technical measures. For instance, a business owner might implement data encryption to protect customer information, while a project manager ensures team members are trained on compliance requirements.
- **Monitor and Audit Compliance:** Regularly monitor compliance with regulations and conduct audits to ensure that controls are effective. This helps identify gaps and areas for improvement. For example, a business owner might conduct regular audits to ensure financial compliance, while a project manager schedules periodic reviews to ensure adherence to project standards.
- **Report and Remediate Non-Compliance:** Develop processes for reporting non-compliance issues and taking corrective actions. This includes reporting to regulatory authorities and implementing remediation plans. For instance, a business owner might report a data breach to relevant authorities and take steps to prevent future incidents, while a project manager addresses non-compliance by adjusting project plans and processes.

Best Practices for Managing Compliance Risks:

- **Stay Informed:** Keep up to date with changes in regulations and industry standards. Both project managers and business owners should subscribe to industry newsletters, attend relevant workshops, and participate in professional networks to stay informed.
- **Foster a Compliance Culture:** Promote a culture of compliance throughout the organization. Encourage employees to adhere to policies and report potential issues. Regular training sessions and clear communication about the importance of compliance can help in building this culture.
- **Leverage Technology:** Use technology to support compliance efforts, such as compliance management systems, automated monitoring tools, and data analytics. For instance, a business owner

might implement a compliance management system to track regulatory changes, while a project manager uses project management software to ensure adherence to project standards.
- **Engage Stakeholders:** Involve legal, compliance, and risk management teams in developing and implementing compliance strategies. For example, a project manager might work with legal teams to ensure contract compliance, while a business owner collaborates with compliance officers to meet regulatory requirements.

All in all..

Effective risk management in advanced topics such as ERM, cybersecurity, agile projects, and regulatory compliance requires a comprehensive and proactive approach. By integrating these practices into their overall risk management framework, project managers and business owners can better navigate the complexities of the modern business environment and achieve their strategic objectives.

11 Tools and Technologies for Risk Management

In the evolving landscape of risk management, leveraging the right tools and technologies can significantly enhance the ability of business owners and project managers to identify, assess, and mitigate risks. In this chapter we present some of the most effective tools and technologies available today.

11.1 Risk Management Software

Risk management software is designed to streamline the process of identifying, assessing, and mitigating risks. These tools offer various features that can help business owners and project managers manage risks more efficiently and effectively.

Key Features of Risk Management Software:

- **Risk Identification and Assessment:** Tools like RiskWatch, LogicManager, and ARM (Active Risk Manager) help in systematically identifying and assessing risks. For example, LogicManager provides risk assessment templates that can be customized to fit the specific needs of a project or business.
- **Risk Reporting and Documentation:** Many software solutions offer comprehensive reporting features. These include dashboards, real-time updates, and automated reports that keep stakeholders informed. For instance, a project manager can use these tools to generate weekly risk reports for the team and stakeholders.
- **Integration with Other Systems:** Risk management software often integrates with other business systems like ERP (Enterprise Resource Planning) and project management tools. This ensures seamless data flow and a holistic view of risks across the organization. For example, integrating with tools like Microsoft

Project or Jira helps in aligning risk management with project timelines and deliverables.
- **Collaboration and Communication:** These tools facilitate better communication and collaboration among team members. Features like shared risk registers, comment sections, and notifications ensure that everyone is on the same page. A business owner can use these features to ensure that all departments are aware of potential risks and are working together to mitigate them.

Benefits of Using Risk Management Software:

- **Efficiency:** Automating risk management processes saves time and reduces the likelihood of human error.
- **Improved Decision-Making:** Access to real-time data and analytics helps in making informed decisions.
- **Scalability:** These tools can scale with the growth of the business, accommodating more complex risk management needs over time.

11.2   Data Analytics in Risk Management

Data analytics plays a crucial role in modern risk management by providing insights that help predict and mitigate risks. For business owners and project managers, leveraging data analytics can lead to more accurate risk assessments and better decision-making.

Key Applications of Data Analytics in Risk Management:

- **Predictive Analytics:** Tools like SAS, IBM SPSS, and Tableau use historical data to predict future risks. For example, a project manager can analyze past project data to identify patterns that might indicate future delays or cost overruns.
- **Risk Quantification:** Data analytics helps quantify risks in financial terms, aiding in better resource allocation. Business owners can use

tools like Palisade's @RISK to perform Monte Carlo simulations, which provide a probabilistic analysis of risk scenarios.
- **Trend Analysis:** Analyzing trends over time can help in identifying emerging risks. Tools like Microsoft Power BI enable businesses to visualize risk data and spot trends that may not be immediately apparent. For example, analyzing customer complaint data might reveal a rising trend in product defects, indicating a potential quality control issue.
- **Real-Time Monitoring:** Real-time data analytics tools help in monitoring risks as they occur. For instance, project managers can use real-time dashboards to track project progress and identify deviations from the plan that may indicate emerging risks.

Benefits of Using Data Analytics in Risk Management:

- **Enhanced Accuracy:** Data-driven insights lead to more accurate risk assessments.
- **Proactive Risk Management:** Predictive analytics and trend analysis help in identifying and mitigating risks before they materialize.
- **Better Resource Allocation:** Quantifying risks in financial terms aids in making informed decisions about where to allocate resources.

11.3 Artificial Intelligence and Machine Learning in Risk Management

Artificial Intelligence (AI) and Machine Learning (ML) are transforming risk management by providing advanced capabilities for identifying, assessing, and mitigating risks. For business owners and project managers, these technologies offer powerful tools to enhance risk management practices.

Key Applications of AI and ML in Risk Management:

- **Automated Risk Identification:** AI algorithms can scan vast amounts of data to identify potential risks that may not be visible through traditional methods. For example, AI-powered tools can analyze social media and news feeds to identify emerging risks related to reputation or market changes.
- **Risk Prediction:** ML models can predict the likelihood of risks occurring based on historical data. For instance, a project manager can use ML models to predict the risk of project delays by analyzing data from previous projects.
- **Anomaly Detection:** AI and ML can detect anomalies in data that might indicate a risk. Tools like Splunk and Anodot use machine learning algorithms to identify unusual patterns that could signify a cybersecurity threat or a financial irregularity.
- **Natural Language Processing (NLP):** NLP helps in analyzing unstructured data such as emails, reports, and social media posts to identify potential risks. For example, AI tools can analyze customer feedback to identify recurring issues that might indicate a product defect.

Benefits of Using AI and ML in Risk Management:

- **Speed:** AI and ML can process and analyze data much faster than humans, enabling quicker identification and assessment of risks.
- **Accuracy:** Machine learning algorithms improve over time, leading to more accurate risk predictions and assessments.
- **Scalability:** AI and ML can handle large volumes of data, making them ideal for organizations of all sizes.

Examples:

- **Automated Risk Identification:** A financial services company uses AI to monitor market trends and identify potential investment risks. The AI system analyzes news articles, social media, and financial reports to provide early warnings of market shifts.
- **Risk Prediction:** A construction firm employs machine learning models to predict project delays. By analyzing data from past

projects, the ML system identifies patterns that may lead to delays, allowing project managers to take proactive measures.
- **Anomaly Detection:** An e-commerce company uses AI-powered anomaly detection to monitor transactions in real-time. The system identifies unusual purchasing patterns that could indicate fraudulent activity, enabling the company to take immediate action.

Leveraging advanced tools and technologies in risk management can significantly enhance the ability of business owners and project managers to manage risks effectively. By integrating risk management software, data analytics, AI, and ML into their risk management practices, they can achieve better risk identification, assessment, and mitigation, leading to more successful projects and business outcomes.

12 Final Thoughts

As presented in this book, risk management is not merely a set of procedures but a vital discipline that plays a crucial role in safeguarding your organization's future. It serves as the foundation for sustainable growth and innovation, ensuring that you can navigate uncertainties with confidence. By diligently applying the principles and practices outlined in this book, you will be well-prepared to manage risks effectively and contribute significantly to your organization's long-term success.

Effective risk management enables you to identify potential threats before they materialize, allowing you to take preemptive measures to mitigate their impact. It also equips you to recognize and exploit opportunities that may arise from uncertain conditions, thereby driving innovation and competitive advantage. A structured approach to risk management ensures that your organization can withstand adverse events while continuing to pursue its strategic goals.

As you implement these risk management strategies, remember that this discipline requires continuous effort and adaptation. The business environment is ever-evolving, and new risks can emerge at any time. Regularly reviewing and updating your risk management processes will keep them relevant and effective. Engage with your team, foster a culture of risk awareness, and encourage open communication to ensure that everyone in the organization understands their role in managing risks.

Furthermore, leveraging technology and data analytics can significantly enhance your risk management capabilities. Advanced tools and software can provide real-time insights, streamline risk assessment processes, and facilitate better decision-making. Stay informed about technological advancements and integrate them into your risk management framework to stay ahead of the curve.

We appreciate your dedication to learning about the fundamentals of risk management through this book. The knowledge and insights you have gained are powerful tools that will help you build a resilient, adaptive, and thriving organization. As you move forward, apply these principles diligently and remain proactive in your approach to managing risks.

Wishing you success in your risk management journey and the continued growth and prosperity of your organization.

Happy risk management!

13   One Last Thing…

I hope you enjoyed this book and found it useful. I'd be very grateful if you'd post a short review on Amazon. Your support does make a difference and your feedback will help us make this book even better.

Other titles available from Marion Parker:

BEYOND THE LAUNCH

ESSENTIAL LESSONS FROM
GROWING A STARTUP

MARION PARKER

www.ingramcontent.com/pod-product-compliance
Lightning Source LLC
Chambersburg PA
CBHW071926210526
45479CB00002B/572